HIGH/SCOPE EDUCATIONAL RESEARCH FOUNDATION

Stone Soup

AND OTHER FAVORITE HIGH/SCOPE RECIPES

Published by
**High/Scope Educational
Research Foundation**

Copyright © High/Scope
Educational Research Foundation
600 North River Street
Ypsilanti, Michigan 48198-2898
313-485-2000

Library of Congress Catalog Number: 97-73440
ISBN: 1-57379-054-0

Edited, Designed, and Manufactured by
Favorite Recipes® Press
an imprint of

FRP™

P.O. Box 305142
Nashville, Tennessee 37230
1-800-358-0560
Manufactured in the United States of America

First Printing: 1997   5,000 copies

Cover Photograph: High/Scope's
headquarters is the Hutchinson House.
Located in Ypsilanti, Michigan, it was built
in 1902 by Shelly Byron Hutchinson,
founder of S&H Green Stamps.

Contents

WHY STONE SOUP?

Stone Soup is a classic folktale of ingenuity and community-building. A hungry boy arrives in a village searching for food and is turned down by everyone he asks because they barely have enough to feed themselves. Finally, he pulls a stone from his pocket and suggests to others in the village that they make "stone soup." He asks for a pot of water and, as the stone simmers, the villagers become intrigued. One by one they contribute a little something to the soup— a carrot, a potato, a bit of salt—until together they have created a magnificent meal. The simple act of sharing brings forth an abundance of food, companionship, and good humor.

As we searched for a title for High/ Scope's cookbook, we wanted to recognize the contributions from our High/Scope friends across the world. Though the teachers and children whose lives we touch are geographically diverse, together we make up a strong community of people committed to high-quality education. And, like stone soup, this cookbook is a collection of favorite morsels from individual kitchens.

We hope that the next time you're feeling hungry you'll find a solution for your meal within these pages. And we hope you enjoy learning a little bit more about High/Scope as you browse.

Enjoy!

W H A T   I S   H I G H / S C O P E ?

Since 1970, the High/Scope Educational Research Foundation has carried out research, curriculum development, training, and publishing related to the education of children and youth. As an independent, nonprofit organization, we strive to make our research findings and services useful and widely accessible, disseminating them through our training and publication programs.

High/Scope's educational approach is based on four guiding principles:

- From birth through adulthood, the individual develops awareness and understanding through active involvement with people, materials, events, and ideas.

- Education is most effective when the individual plans, carries out, and reflects on intentional activities.

- A variety of developmentally appropriate active learning experiences contributes to the individual's intellectual, social, emotional, and physical development.

- Consistent support and respect for personal decision-making strengthen the individual's confidence, self-control, and sense of personal effectiveness and responsibility.

High/Scope's educational practices have had a positive impact on children and families worldwide. In the United States, close to half a million children in preschools, child care centers, and elementary schools benefit from programs using the High/Scope active learning approach. Student teachers and visitors from around the world are able to observe a model High/Scope program in action at our Demonstration Preschool in Ypsilanti, Michigan, rated by *Child Magazine* as one of the nation's ten best early childhood classrooms.

Without a doubt, high-quality early childhood programs that emphasize children's initiative give many young children educational and social skills that they are able to build upon throughout their lives. The cycle of school failure, unemployment, crime, family instability, and welfare begins early in life.

In fact, the High/Scope Perry Preschool Project—a 30-year study of preschool's effects—has demonstrated that taxpayers save over $7 in future costs for each dollar invested in high-quality early childhood programs.

To bring High/Scope's educational approach to communities worldwide, we have developed a system of teacher training that combines active workshop experiences with on-site work with teachers and children. The International High/Scope Registry, established in 1989, ensures the quality and consistency of High/Scope training by certifying teachers, teacher-trainers, and programs. The 1,300 teacher-trainers certified so far by High/Scope train more than 30,000 teachers and child care providers annually. We continually revise and expand our training programs to meet the needs of today's teachers and caregivers.

Our evolving teacher-training programs—conducted at our headquarters in Ypsilanti, at locations around the country, and on site in other countries—have enabled us to expand the capacity of both preschool and elementary school teachers to provide developmentally appropriate instruction in their classroom, home, and center settings. High/Scope Institutes are also established in the United Kingdom, the Netherlands, Singapore, and Mexico.

At the elementary level, educators have recognized the positive effects of the High/Scope Curriculum on students' literacy skills, achievement scores, and problem-solving abilities. In addition, we have helped teachers at a dozen preschool and elementary sites nationwide apply computer technology and the High/Scope educational approach in their classrooms.

Publishing is another way that High/Scope reaches out to inform those who work in, or make decisions about, programs for children and families. High/Scope Press produces research reports, books, monographs, newsletters, videos, curriculum materials, assessment instruments, and recorded music. High/Scope curriculum and training materials in infant and toddler education, preschool education, music and movement, elementary education, and adolescent programs bring our active learning approach to a wider audience.

Throughout the world, social and economic changes have led to a greater need for early childhood services. These changes, and the growing awareness of the importance of the early years in assuring success throughout one's life, have increased the need for comprehensive information to guide policy decisions and program development. In response, High/Scope has taken the lead in coordinating research both within the United States and internationally in order to develop new knowledge about education and human development.

High/Scope's educational leadership also extends to our high schools, where increasing numbers of low-income youths of varying backgrounds are dropping out because of low personal expectations and inadequate support. We are addressing the challenge of this individual and societal loss throughout our month-long residential Institute for IDEAS. This program, which boosts the achievement and career aspirations of disadvantaged teens, includes follow-up service-learning projects in the students' communities. The Institute is now being replicated around the country in a variety of settings and populations.

As High/Scope's programs and services develop and expand, their positive impact will continue to be felt in our schools and communities. High/Scope will continue to seek a leadership role, informing and educating those whose work touches the lives of our youngest citizens.

High/Scope's preschool programs emphasize active learning.

HOLIDAY SHRIMP DIP

YIELD: 20 SERVINGS

1 (6-ounce) can small cocktail shrimp

Juice of 2 lemons

3 tablespoons mayonnaise, or to taste

1½ tablespoons chili sauce or catsup, or to taste

⅛ teaspoon Tabasco sauce (optional)

Celery seeds to taste (optional)

Paprika to taste (optional)

Melba toast

An appetizer that goes well with all festive food. It has a mild, deliciously different flavor that appeals to both children and adults. This recipe comes from the 1950s—a time when people weren't embarrassed about using canned ingredients.

Rinse and drain the shrimp. Soak the shrimp in the lemon juice in a bowl in the refrigerator for 6 hours to overnight.

Drain the shrimp, reserving the lemon juice. Mash the shrimp in the bowl. Add ½ of the reserved lemon juice, mayonnaise and chili sauce and mix well. Add as much of the remaining lemon juice as is needed for the desired consistency. Stir in the Tabasco sauce and celery seeds.

Spoon into a serving bowl. Sprinkle with the paprika. Serve with the melba toast.

NANCY BRICKMAN–HIGH/SCOPE EDITOR   YPSILANTI, MICHIGAN

FOOD FOR THOUGHT

Don't try to improve upon this recipe by using fresh or frozen shrimp. I've tried it, and it doesn't work.

CRAB MEAT DIP

Beat the cream cheese in a mixer bowl until smooth. Stir in the crab meat, garlic, mayonnaise, dry mustard, confectioners' sugar, seasoned salt and wine. Spoon into a 1¹/₂-quart chafing dish. Heat until heated through.

Serve with the crackers.

EMILY KOEPP–HIGH/SCOPE DIRECTOR OF MARKETING AND FUND DEVELOPMENT
YPSILANTI, MICHIGAN

FOOD FOR THOUGHT

May freeze this dip and then reheat in a chafing dish before serving.

24 ounces cream cheese,
   softened
 2 (4-ounce) cans crab meat,
   drained, flaked
 1 clove of garlic, crushed
¹/₂ cup mayonnaise
 2 teaspoons dry mustard
 2 teaspoons confectioners'
   sugar
   Seasoned salt to taste
¹/₄ cup white wine
   Assorted crackers

HOT ARTICHOKE SPREAD

Drain the artichoke hearts. Chop the artichoke hearts and place in a bowl. Stir in the Parmesan cheese, mayonnaise and garlic powder. Spoon into a greased ramekin. Bake at 350 degrees for 20 minutes or until bubbly.

Serve with the crackers or chips.

SKIP SACKETT   FONTANA, WISCONSIN

 1 (14-ounce) can artichoke
   hearts
 1 cup grated Parmesan
   cheese
 1 cup mayonnaise
   Garlic powder to taste
   Assorted crackers or chips

YIELD: 4 TO 6 SERVINGS

1 cup sugar

1/3 cup packed brown sugar

1/2 cup water

1 teaspoon (scant) salt

1 tablespoon cinnamon

1 tablespoon vanilla extract

2 1/2 to 3 cups walnut halves

S U G A R E D   W A L N U T S

Bring the sugar, brown sugar, water and salt to a boil in a saucepan. Cook over high heat to 234 to 240 degrees on a candy thermometer, soft-ball stage, stirring constantly. Remove from heat. Stir in the cinnamon and vanilla. Add the walnuts 1/2 cup at a time, stirring until well coated after each addition.

Pour onto waxed paper. Let stand until cool enough to handle. Separate into individual pieces. Store in an airtight container.

FRIEND OF HIGH/SCOPE

Sweet Indian Pickles

YIELD: 32 SERVINGS

Place the sliced cucumbers in a sterilized 1-gallon glass jar. Combine the sugar, vinegar, salt, celery seeds, green pepper and onion in a blender container. Process for 1 minute. Pour over the cucumbers.

Chill, covered, in the refrigerator for at least 24 hours.

High/Scope Camp and Conference Center   Clinton, Michigan

FOOD FOR THOUGHT

The longer the cucumbers marinate in the brine, the better the pickles.

8 cups sliced unpeeled cucumbers

2 cups sugar

1 cup apple cider vinegar

2 tablespoons (heaping) salt

1 tablespoon celery seeds

1 cup chopped green bell pepper

1 cup chopped onion

HOT COCOA

YIELD: 4 servings

1/4 cup plus 2 tablespoons
  baking cocoa
1/2 cup sugar
1/8 teaspoon salt
 4 cups milk

Hot Cocoa is a wintertime MUST at our house!

Combine the baking cocoa, sugar, salt and milk in a 2-quart saucepan. Cook for 5 minutes or until heated through, stirring constantly. Do not boil. Remove from heat. Beat with a rotary beater until foamy.

Ladle into mugs and serve immediately.

JAN GIFFORD—HIGH/SCOPE ELEMENTARY DIVISION SECRETARY
YPSILANTI, MICHIGAN

HOMEMADE CREAM CORDIAL

Combine the condensed milk, liqueur, whipping cream and eggs in a blender container. Process until smooth.

Serve over ice in serving glasses.

JAN GIFFORD–HIGH/SCOPE ELEMENTARY DIVISION SECRETARY
YPSILANTI, MICHIGAN

1 (14-ounce) can sweetened condensed milk

1¹/₄ cups favorite liqueur, such as almond, coffee, orange or mint

1 cup whipping cream

4 eggs

FOOD FOR THOUGHT

May store, tightly covered, in the refrigerator for up to 1 month. Stir well before serving. To avoid raw eggs that may carry salmonella, use an equivalent amount of pasteurized egg substitute. You may also bring 2 inches of water to a boil in a small saucepan and turn off heat. Lower the eggs carefully into the water and let stand for 1 to 1¹/₂ minutes. Remove the eggs carefully. Let stand until slightly cooled before removing the shell.

YIELD: 4 TO 6 SERVINGS

1 cup salad oil

$^1/_4$ cup sugar

$^1/_4$ cup vinegar

2 teaspoons salt

$^1/_8$ teaspoon pepper

1 package mixed salad
greens

1 red onion, thinly sliced

1 (11-ounce) can mandarin
oranges, drained

Glazed Almonds

MANDARIN ORANGE SALAD WITH GLAZED ALMONDS

Combine the salad oil, sugar, vinegar, salt and pepper in a container with a tightfitting lid. Cover and shake well until the sugar is dissolved. Add the dressing to the salad greens in a salad bowl and toss well.

Place the salad on individual salad plates. Arrange red onion slices on the top of each salad. Place mandarin oranges at the edge of each salad. Sprinkle with Glazed Almonds.

GLAZED ALMONDS

1 tablespoon margarine

1 cup slivered almonds

3 to 4 tablespoons sugar

Melt the margarine in a skillet. Stir in the almonds and sugar. Cook over medium heat until the almonds are golden brown, stirring constantly.

FRIEND OF HIGH/SCOPE

TROPICAL FRUIT SALAD

Combine the mandarin oranges, pineapple, coconut and marshmallows in a bowl and mix well. Stir in the sour cream. Spoon into a salad bowl.

Chill, covered, until serving time. Garnish with maraschino cherries just before serving.

FRIEND OF HIGH/SCOPE

YIELD: 4 TO 6 SERVINGS

1 (8-ounce) can mandarin oranges, drained
1 (8-ounce) can crushed pineapple, drained
1 cup shredded coconut
1 cup miniature marshmallows
1 cup sour cream
  Maraschino cherries

YIELD: 4 SERVINGS

1/2 cup vegetable oil

2 tablespoons vinegar

1 tablespoon honey

3/4 teaspoon salt

1/8 teaspoon pepper

4 drops of red pepper sauce,
   or to taste

3 cups chopped cooked
   turkey or chicken

1 1/2 cups seedless grapes

1/4 cup sliced green onions
   with tops

1/4 cup chopped green bell
   pepper

1 (8-ounce) can water
   chestnuts, drained,
   chopped

3 cups torn lettuce

2 oranges, peeled, cut into
   sections

1/2 cup toasted slivered
   almonds

FRUITED TURKEY SALAD

Combine the vegetable oil, vinegar, honey, salt, pepper and red pepper sauce in a container with a tightfitting lid. Cover and shake well. Combine the turkey, grapes, green onions, green pepper and water chestnuts in a bowl and mix well. Add the salad dressing and toss well. Chill, covered, for 2 hours or longer.

Add the lettuce and oranges to the chilled salad just before serving and toss well. Spoon onto lettuce-lined salad plates and sprinkle with the toasted almonds.

HIGH/SCOPE CAMP AND CONFERENCE CENTER   CLINTON, MICHIGAN

CASHEW CHICKEN SALAD

Mix the brown mustard, orange juice, pepper and mayonnaise in a small bowl. Combine the chicken, red peppers, celery and green onions in a large bowl. Stir in the mustard dressing. Chill, covered, in the refrigerator until serving time.

Stir in the cashews just before serving. Spoon onto lettuce-lined salad plates.

HIGH/SCOPE CAMP AND CONFERENCE CENTER   CLINTON, MICHIGAN

1/4 cup brown mustard

1/4 cup orange juice

1/2 teaspoon pepper

1 cup mayonnaise

2 1/2 cups chopped cooked chicken

2 small red bell peppers, chopped

1 1/2 cups chopped celery

1/2 cup chopped green onions

1 1/2 cups whole cashews

YIELD: 4 SERVINGS

2 chicken breast fillets,
  cooked, shredded

1/2 head cabbage, thinly sliced

2 green onions, chopped

2 tablespoons toasted
  sesame seeds

2 tablespoons toasted
  slivered almonds

1 package ramen noodles,
  crumbled

1/2 cup salad oil

3 tablespoons vinegar

2 tablespoons sugar

  Lemon juice to taste

1 teaspoon salt

1 teaspoon pepper

CABBAGE AND CHICKEN SALAD

Combine the chicken, cabbage, green onions, sesame seeds, almonds and ramen noodles in a bowl and mix well. Mix the salad oil, vinegar, sugar, lemon juice, salt and pepper in a bowl. Add to the chicken mixture and mix well.

Chill, covered, in the refrigerator.

ERICA SAMPSON   LANSING, MICHIGAN

VEGETABLE PASTA SALAD

YIELD: VARIABLE

1 pound spaghetti or linguini, cooked, drained

Any combination of fresh chopped or sliced vegetables such as broccoli, cauliflower, mushrooms, carrots, celery, red bell pepper, green bell pepper, yellow bell pepper, tiny yellow squash, tiny zucchini or green onions

Dry-pack sun-dried tomatoes to taste

Grated Parmesan cheese to taste

Italian salad dressing to taste

Combine the cooled spaghetti, fresh vegetables, sun-dried tomatoes and Parmesan cheese in a large bowl and toss until mixed well. Add the salad dressing and toss well. Chill in the refrigerator until serving time.

HIGH/SCOPE CAMP AND CONFERENCE CENTER   CLINTON, MICHIGAN

BROCCOLI SALAD

YIELD: 4 TO 6 SERVINGS

1 cup mayonnaise

1/3 cup sugar

2 tablespoons vinegar

1/8 teaspoon salt

1 1/2 pounds broccoli, cut into florets

1 cup chopped red onion

10 slices bacon, crisp-fried, crumbled

1 cup raisins

1 cup sunflower seed kernels

1 (8-ounce) can water chestnuts, drained

Combine the mayonnaise, sugar, vinegar and salt in a bowl and mix well. Chill, covered, in the refrigerator.

Combine the broccoli, red onion, bacon, raisins, sunflower seed kernels and water chestnuts in a bowl and mix well. Add the chilled salad dressing and toss well. Serve immediately.

HIGH/SCOPE CAMP AND CONFERENCE CENTER   CLINTON, MICHIGAN

FOOD FOR THOUGHT

May reduce sugar to 1/2 cup in the dressing and decrease the bacon to 7 slices.

BROCCOLI AND TOMATO SALAD

Combine the broccoli, black olives, red onion, tomatoes, celery, water chestnuts and oregano in a large bowl and mix well. Prepare the Italian salad dressing mix using the package directions. Add to the broccoli mixture and toss to mix well.

Marinate, covered, in the refrigerator for several hours to overnight.

MARGY SHOUSE   YPSILANTI, MICHIGAN

YIELD: 4 TO 6 SERVINGS

1 *head broccoli, cut into florets*

1 *(4-ounce) can sliced black olives*

1 *red onion, sliced*

1 *pint cherry tomatoes, cut into quarters*

2 *ribs celery, sliced*

1 *(8-ounce) can sliced water chestnuts, drained*

1/4 *teaspoon oregano*

1 *package Italian salad dressing mix*

YIELD: 8 TO 10 SERVINGS

TWENTY-FOUR CARROT SALAD

2 pounds carrots, peeled,
  cut into 1-inch slices
  (about 5 cups)

1 (10-ounce) can tomato
  soup

3/4 cup cider or white vinegar

3/4 cup sugar

1/2 cup vegetable oil

1 teaspoon prepared
  mustard

1/4 teaspoon pepper

1 large onion, cut into
  medium slivers
  (about 1 cup)

1 large green bell pepper,
  chopped (about 1 cup)

Bring the carrots to a boil in water to cover in a saucepan. Boil for 5 minutes and drain. Let stand until cool.

Blend the soup, vinegar, sugar, vegetable oil, mustard and pepper in a large bowl. Add the carrots, onion and green pepper and mix well.

Chill, tightly covered, overnight.

HIGH/SCOPE CAMP AND CONFERENCE CENTER   CLINTON, MICHIGAN

CHICK-PEA AND ARTICHOKE SALAD

Combine the chick-peas, artichoke hearts, tomatoes, green onions, Parmesan cheese, garlic, basil and parsley in a bowl and mix well. Stir in the olive oil, red wine vinegar, lemon juice and salt and pepper. Adjust the seasonings to taste.

Marinate, covered, in the refrigerator until serving time.

HIGH/SCOPE CAMP AND CONFERENCE CENTER   CLINTON, MICHIGAN

YIELD: 10 TO 12 SERVINGS

3 (16-ounce) cans chick-peas or garbanzo beans, drained

3 (14-ounce) cans artichoke hearts, drained

1 pound tomatoes, seeded, chopped

1 cup chopped green onions

1/4 cup grated Parmesan cheese

2 teaspoons minced garlic, or to taste

2 teaspoons basil

2 teaspoons parsley

1/4 cup olive oil

2 tablespoons red wine vinegar

2 teaspoons lemon juice

Salt and pepper to taste

LAYERED VEGETABLE SALAD

Chopped lettuce

1 (10-ounce) package frozen green peas, thawed

1 (8-ounce) can sliced water chestnuts, drained

Chopped onion

2 cups mayonnaise

3 tomatoes, chopped, drained

5 or 6 hard-cooked eggs, grated

6 slices bacon, crisp-fried, crumbled

Salt and pepper to taste

Layer the lettuce, green peas, water chestnuts, onion, mayonnaise, tomatoes, hard-cooked eggs and bacon in the order listed in a 9x13-inch dish. Sprinkle with salt and pepper to taste.

Chill, covered, in the refrigerator for 8 to 10 hours before serving.

FRIEND OF HIGH/SCOPE

CRUNCHY GREEN PEA SALAD

Combine the green peas, celery, cauliflower, green onions and cashews in a bowl and mix well. Stir in the sour cream and ranch salad dressing. Spoon into a serving bowl. Sprinkle with the bacon.

Chill, covered, before serving.

FRIEND OF HIGH/SCOPE

YIELD: 4 TO 6 SERVINGS

1 (10-ounce) package frozen green peas, thawed
1 cup chopped celery
1 cup chopped cauliflower
1/4 cup chopped green onions
1 cup chopped cashews
1/2 cup sour cream
1 cup ranch salad dressing
Crumbled crisp-fried bacon

YIELD: 4 TO 6 SERVINGS

1/2 teaspoon salt

Freshly ground pepper

6 tablespoons safflower oil

2 tablespoons vinegar

3 cups sliced boiled potatoes

3 tablespoons finely chopped onion

1 cup finely diced celery

3/4 cup Hellman's mayonnaise

3 tablespoons evaporated milk

2 or 3 hard-cooked eggs, coarsely chopped

AUNT IDA'S POTATO SALAD

This is my great-aunt's potato salad recipe. Marinating the potatoes overnight and adding the evaporated milk to the mayonnaise make this recipe so good.

Mix salt and pepper in a large bowl. Stir in the oil with a fork. Add the vinegar gradually, stirring well after each addition. Add the potatoes, onion and celery and mix gently until the vegetables are thoroughly coated, being careful not to break the potato slices.

Marinate, covered, in the refrigerator for 2 hours to overnight. Mix the mayonnaise and evaporated milk in a small bowl. Fold into the potato mixture. Stir in the hard-cooked eggs. Chill, covered, in the refrigerator until serving time.

ANNE HUDON–HIGH/SCOPE CONFERENCE COORDINATOR AND ASSISTANT TO THE REGISTRAR
YPSILANTI, MICHIGAN

FOOD FOR THOUGHT

This recipe may be doubled, but do not double the amount of onion or celery.

Tossed Romaine and Walnut Salad

Yield: 4 to 6 servings

1/2 cup honey
1 cup vegetable oil
1/4 cup vinegar
1/2 teaspoon dry mustard
8 cups torn romaine lettuce
1 cup chopped lightly toasted walnuts

Combine the honey, oil, vinegar and dry mustard in a small bowl and mix well. Pour over the lettuce in a salad bowl just before serving and toss well.

Sprinkle the walnuts over the top and serve immediately.

High/Scope Camp and Conference Center   Clinton, Michigan

FRESH SPINACH SALAD

YIELD: 10 TO 12 SERVINGS

1 cup salad oil

1/2 cup dark vinegar

3/4 cup sugar

1/2 cup catsup

2 teaspoons salt

1 (12-ounce) package fresh
    spinach

1 (8-ounce) can water
    chestnuts, drained,
    chopped

1 (14-ounce) can bean
    sprouts, drained

3 hard-cooked eggs, sliced

4 ounces bacon, crisp-fried,
    crumbled

1 large onion, thinly sliced

Combine the salad oil, vinegar, sugar, catsup and salt in a bowl and mix well. Store, covered, in the refrigerator.

Rinse the spinach and drain well. Tear the spinach into bite-size pieces into a salad bowl. Add the water chestnuts and bean sprouts and toss well. Layer the hard-cooked eggs, bacon and onion over the top of the salad.

Chill, covered, in the refrigerator until serving time. Add the dressing to the salad just before serving.

FRIEND OF HIGH/SCOPE

ORIENTAL SPINACH SALAD

YIELD: 14 TO 16 SERVINGS

Rinse the spinach and drain well. Tear the spinach into bite-size pieces into a salad bowl. Chill, loosely covered, in the refrigerator.

Combine the vegetable oil, catsup, vinegar, sugar, salt, Worcestershire sauce and onion in a bowl and mix well.

Reserve a small amount of the hard-cooked eggs and bacon for garnish. Add the water chestnuts, remaining hard-cooked eggs and remaining bacon to the spinach and toss well. Add the dressing and toss well. Garnish with the reserved hard-cooked eggs and bacon. Serve immediately.

HIGH/SCOPE CAMP AND CONFERENCE CENTER   CLINTON, MICHIGAN

- 2 (12-ounce) packages fresh spinach, trimmed
- 1 cup vegetable oil
- 1/3 cup catsup
- 1/4 cup vinegar
- 3/4 cup sugar
- 1 teaspoon salt, or to taste
- 1 tablespoon Worcestershire sauce
- 1 small onion, slivered
- 4 hard-cooked eggs, sliced
- 8 ounces bacon, crisp-fried, crumbled
- 2 (8-ounce) cans water chestnuts, drained

Yield: 4 to 6 servings

1/4 cup safflower or vegetable
   oil
2 tablespoons salad vinegar
1 tablespoon sugar, or to
   taste
2 tablespoons finely chopped
   green onions
1 teaspoon salt, or to taste
1/8 teaspoon pepper
1/8 teaspoon Tabasco sauce
1 (12-ounce) package
   spinach, trimmed
1 pint strawberries
2 tablespoons toasted
   sesame seeds

Spinach and Strawberry Salad

Combine the oil, vinegar, sugar, green onions, salt, pepper and Tabasco sauce in a container with a tightfitting lid. Cover and shake well until the sugar and salt are dissolved. Chill in the refrigerator.

Rinse the spinach and pat dry. Tear the spinach into bite-size pieces into a salad bowl. Chill, loosely covered, in the refrigerator. Rinse the strawberries and remove the caps. Cut the strawberries into slices.

Add the sesame seeds and dressing to the spinach and toss well. Add the strawberries and toss until the strawberries are coated with the dressing. Serve immediately.

High/Scope Camp and Conference Center   Clinton, Michigan

GLORIFIED TOMATO ASPIC

YIELD: 6 TO 8 SERVINGS

Heat the tomato juice in a saucepan until heated through. Add the gelatin, stirring until dissolved. Stir in the vinegar and onion. Pour into a bowl and chill until partially set. Fold in the avocados.

Line an oiled ring mold with the artichoke hearts. Add the partially set gelatin mixture. Chill until firm. Unmold onto a serving plate. Serve with a mixture of the mayonnaise and horseradish.

SKIP SACKETT   FONTANA, WISCONSIN

2 cups tomato juice

1 (6-ounce) package lemon gelatin

1 tablespoon tarragon vinegar

1 onion, grated

2 avocados, cut up

1 (14-ounce) can artichoke hearts, drained

3 tablespoons mayonnaise

1 tablespoon prepared horseradish

ITALIAN SALAD DRESSING

YIELD: 8 TO 12 SERVINGS

2 cups olive oil

3/4 cup vinegar

1/2 cup grated fresh Parmesan
cheese

1 1/2 tablespoons sugar

1 tablespoon salt

1/4 tablespoon celery seeds

3/4 teaspoon white or black
pepper

3/4 teaspoon dry mustard

1/4 teaspoon paprika

2 cloves of garlic

Combine the olive oil, vinegar, Parmesan cheese, sugar, salt, celery seeds, white pepper, dry mustard, paprika and garlic in a container with a tightfitting lid. Cover and shake well. Adjust the seasonings.

Chill in the refrigerator. Shake well before serving.

HIGH/SCOPE CAMP AND CONFERENCE CENTER   CLINTON, MICHIGAN

38

MAISON DRESSING

YIELD: 18 TO 20 SERVINGS

Whisk the mayonnaise, chicken stock, garlic and white pepper in a bowl. Pour into a tightly covered container.

Chill, covered, in the refrigerator.

HIGH/SCOPE CAMP AND CONFERENCE CENTER   CLINTON, MICHIGAN

FOOD FOR THOUGHT

Very good served over tossed salad greens and vegetables. It may also be used as a vegetable dip. The chicken stock used in this recipe can be made from chicken base.

4 cups mayonnaise or mayonnaise-type salad dressing

1 cup chicken stock

1 tablespoon granulated garlic

1 teaspoon white pepper

1 cup vegetable oil

1/2 cup orange juice

1/4 cup wine vinegar

1/4 cup sugar

2 tablespoons lemon juice

1 teaspoon (heaping) grated orange peel

MANDARIN ORANGE SALAD DRESSING

Mix the vegetable oil, orange juice, wine vinegar, sugar, lemon juice and orange peel in a bowl and mix well.

Store in a tightly covered container in the refrigerator. Stir the dressing before serving.

HIGH/SCOPE CAMP AND CONFERENCE CENTER   CLINTON, MICHIGAN

FOOD FOR THOUGHT

Serve this wonderful salad dressing over fresh torn spinach or other salad greens. Sprinkle the salad with drained mandarin oranges and toasted sliced almonds just before serving.

APPLESAUCE RAISIN BREAD

YIELD: 12 SERVINGS

1$^1/2$ cups thick applesauce
1 cup sugar
$^1/2$ cup melted margarine
2$^1/2$ cups flour
2 teaspoons baking soda
1 tablespoon cinnamon
1 teaspoon ground cloves
1 cup raisins

Combine the applesauce, sugar and margarine in a bowl and mix well. Stir in a mixture of flour, baking soda, cinnamon and cloves. Fold in the raisins. Pour into a greased 5x9-inch loaf pan.

Bake at 350 degrees for 1 hour or until the loaf tests done.

HIGH/SCOPE CAMP AND CONFERENCE CENTER   CLINTON, MICHIGAN

YIELD: 12 SERVINGS

1 1/2 cups flour
2 teaspoons baking powder
1/2 teaspoon baking soda
1 teaspoon salt
2 eggs
1/3 cup milk
1/3 cup vegetable oil
1/2 cup sugar
3/4 cup rolled oats
1 cup mashed bananas
1/2 cup chopped walnuts

BANANA BREAD

Mix the flour, baking powder, baking soda and salt together. Combine the eggs, milk, vegetable oil and sugar in a bowl and mix well. Add the flour mixture and mix just until blended. Stir in the oats. Add the bananas and walnuts and stir just until blended. Pour into a greased 5x9-inch loaf pan.

Bake at 350 degrees for 55 to 60 minutes or until a wooden pick inserted in the center comes out clean.

HIGH/SCOPE CAMP AND CONFERENCE CENTER   CLINTON, MICHIGAN

PUMPKIN BREAD

Mix the all-purpose flour, whole wheat flour, baking powder, baking soda, salt and spices in a large bowl. Combine the pumpkin, sugar, vegetable oil, eggs and vanilla in a large mixer bowl and beat well. Add the flour mixture gradually, beating constantly. Do not over mix. Pour into 9 greased 5x9-inch loaf pans.

   Bake in a preheated 350-degree oven for 1 hour or until the loaves test done. Invert onto wire racks to cool. Let the loaves cool completely before cutting into slices.

KASENA DAILEY   BEAVERTON, OREGON

FOOD FOR THOUGHT

Serve slices of Pumpkin Bread with cream cheese, raisins and cherries and have children make faces on their own pieces of bread.

12 cups all-purpose flour

8 cups whole wheat flour

3 tablespoons baking powder

3 tablespoons baking soda

1 tablespoon salt

Cinnamon, nutmeg and allspice to taste

1 (No. 10) can pumpkin (106 ounces or 13 cups)

9 cups sugar

3 cups vegetable oil

24 eggs

1/4 cup vanilla extract

YIELD: 12 SERVINGS

2 teaspoons baking soda
1 tablespoon hot water
2 cups buttermilk
3/4 cup sugar
1 egg
1 teaspoon salt
2 3/4 cups graham flour
1/2 cup chopped nuts

GRAHAM BROWN BREAD

This is a very delicious nutritious bread.

Dissolve the baking soda in the hot water in a cup. Add to the buttermilk and mix well. Combine the sugar, egg, salt and buttermilk mixture in a large bowl and mix well. Stir in the flour. Fold in the nuts. The batter will be thick. Spoon into a greased 6x9-inch loaf pan.

Bake at 350 degrees for 1 hour or until a wooden pick inserted in the center comes out clean. Cool slightly in the pan. Invert onto a wire rack to cool completely.

MARGARET ANN KILDAU   YPSILANTI, MICHIGAN

FOOD FOR THOUGHT

Graham flour is whole wheat flour that is slightly coarser than regular grind.

DILLY BREAD

Dissolve the yeast in the warm water and set aside. Combine the cottage cheese, sugar, dried onion, margarine, dillweed, salt, baking soda and eggs in a large bowl and beat well. Add the yeast mixture and mix well. Add the flour gradually, stirring in enough to form a stiff dough.

Knead on a lightly floured surface until smooth and elastic. Place in a greased bowl and rub the surface with additional margarine. Let rise, covered, until doubled in bulk. Punch the dough down and knead again.

Divide the dough into 2 portions. Shape each portion into a loaf. Place in two greased 5x9-inch loaf pans. Let rise until doubled in bulk.

Bake at 350 degrees for 30 to 40 minutes or until golden brown.

HIGH/SCOPE CAMP AND CONFERENCE CENTER   CLINTON, MICHIGAN

2 envelopes dry yeast
1/2 cup warm water
2 cups creamed large-curd cottage cheese
1/4 cup sugar
2 tablespoons dried minced onion
2 tablespoons margarine
2 tablespoons dillweed
4 teaspoons salt
1/2 teaspoon baking soda
2 eggs, beaten
4 to 5 cups flour

YIELD: 3 TO 4 LOAVES

2 tablespoons yeast
1 cup warm water
1 cup yellow cornmeal
1 cup All-Bran cereal
1 cup rolled oats
1/2 cup shortening
1/2 cup honey
2 tablespoons salt
4 cups hot water
2 cups whole wheat flour
6 cups all-purpose flour

MIKE'S OATMEAL BREAD

Dissolve the yeast in 1 cup warm water and set aside. Combine the cornmeal, cereal, oats, shortening, honey and salt in a large mixer bowl. Add 4 cups hot water and beat well. Stir in some of the whole wheat flour. Add the yeast mixture and the remaining whole wheat flour and mix well. Beat in enough of the all-purpose flour to form a stiff dough. Let rise, covered, until doubled in bulk.

Turn the dough onto a floured surface and divide the dough into portions. Knead each portion about 20 times. Shape each portion into a loaf. Place in greased 5x9-inch loaf pans.

Bake at 350 degrees for 35 minutes or until the loaves sound hollow when lightly tapped.

HIGH/SCOPE CAMP AND CONFERENCE CENTER   CLINTON, MICHIGAN

FROSTED FRENCH BREAD

YIELD: 12 SERVINGS

Trim the crust from the bread. Cut a row of x's in the top of the loaf. Insert the Swiss cheese in the slits.

Beat the butter, margarine, lemon juice, onion, dry mustard and seasoned salt in a mixer bowl until smooth and creamy. Spread over the bread loaf. Sprinkle with Parmesan cheese.

Chill, covered, in the refrigerator for 30 minutes or freeze until the topping is firm. Place on a baking sheet. Bake at 350 degrees for 30 minutes.

FRIEND OF HIGH/SCOPE

1 loaf French bread

12 ounces Swiss cheese, sliced

1/2 cup butter

1/2 cup margarine

1 tablespoon lemon juice

1 teaspoon minced onion

1 teaspoon dry mustard

1 teaspoon seasoned salt

Grated Parmesan cheese to taste

YIELD: 12 SERVINGS

SAUCY PEPPERONI BREAD

My co-workers request that I make this recipe for special occasions.

1 loaf frozen bread dough, thawed

Melted butter to taste

Favorite pizza sauce to taste

Grated Parmesan cheese to taste

Shredded mozzarella cheese to taste

Pepperoni slices

Roll the dough into a rectangle on a lightly floured surface. Sprinkle lightly with melted butter. Spread a thin layer of the sauce over the dough. Sprinkle with the Parmesan cheese and mozzarella cheese. Cover the top with pepperoni slices.

Roll as for a jelly roll, pinching the ends to seal. Place in a greased and floured 5x9-inch loaf pan. Bake at 400 degrees for 30 minutes or until golden brown.

KELLY HAMILTON   PITTSBURGH, PENNSYLVANIA

PEPPERONI BREAD

YIELD: 6 SERVINGS

Roll the bread dough on a baking sheet until the entire surface is covered. Beat the eggs, garlic salt and oregano in a bowl. Spread 3/4 of the mixture over the dough. Layer the pepperoni and mozzarella cheese over the top.

Roll as for a jelly roll from the long side, sealing the ends. Coat the top and sides with the remaining egg mixture. Bake at 350 degrees for 20 to 30 minutes or until golden brown.

BECKY CARSWELL   WOODBRIDGE, VIRGINIA

1 loaf frozen bread dough, thawed

2 eggs

Garlic salt to taste

Oregano to taste

Pepperoni slices

Shredded mozzarella cheese to taste

YIELD: 40 SERVINGS

1 (10-ounce) package frozen
   chopped spinach
1 cup flour
1 teaspoon salt
1 teaspoon baking powder
2 eggs, beaten
1 cup milk
1/4 cup melted butter
1/2 cup chopped onion
1 pound shredded Cheddar
   cheese

SPINACH BROWNIES

This is also good served for a breakfast or brunch.

Thaw the spinach and drain well. Sift the flour, salt and baking powder into a large bowl. Add the eggs, milk and butter and mix well. Stir in the onion, cheese and drained spinach. Spoon into a 9x13-inch baking pan.

Bake at 350 degrees for 30 minutes. Cool slightly before cutting into bars.

BECKY CARSWELL   WOODBRIDGE, VIRGINIA

Apple Cinnamon Muffins

Mix the flour, nonfat dry milk, sugar, baking powder, 1/2 teaspoon cinnamon and salt in a large bowl. Beat the egg and water in a bowl. Stir in the apple and margarine. Add to the flour mixture all at once and stir just until moistened. The batter will be very stiff.

Fill 12 greased or paper-lined muffin cups 2/3 full. Mix the nuts, brown sugar and 1/2 teaspoon cinnamon in a bowl. Sprinkle over the batter.

Bake at 375 degrees for 15 to 20 minutes or until the muffins test done. Invert immediately onto wire racks to cool.

Jan Gifford–High/Scope Elementary Division Secretary
Ypsilanti, Michigan

- 1 1/2 cups flour
- 1/2 cup nonfat dry milk
- 1/3 cup sugar
- 2 teaspoons baking powder
- 1/2 teaspoon cinnamon
- 1/2 teaspoon salt
- 1 egg
- 1/2 cup water
- 1 cup chopped peeled Cortland or Granny Smith apple
- 1/4 cup melted margarine
- 1/3 cup chopped nuts
- 1/4 cup packed brown sugar
- 1/2 teaspoon cinnamon

M I X - A N D - M A T C H   M U F F I N S

YIELD: 12 SERVINGS

1 egg, or 2 egg whites

1/4 cup canola oil

1 cup juice or skim milk

1/2 cup sugar

2 cups whole wheat flour

1/4 cup wheat germ

1 tablespoon baking powder

1/2 teaspoon salt

I started baking muffins twenty-five years ago when a visitor to Michigan brought me a bag of stone-ground whole wheat flour and a bag of stone-ground cornmeal from a restored nineteenth-century mill in the Washington, D.C. area. I happened to have some blueberries on hand and thus my first muffin recipe was born. Since then, almost any edible and natural ingredient has been tried in my muffin pans with (admittedly) varying degrees of success. I've included the favorite variations of my family and friends here.

As a researcher, I encourage all cooks to be experimental! Be inventive and create your own muffins. Use any combination of grains, fresh or dried fruit, nuts and seeds, and spices to create your own favorite muffins.

Beat the egg in a mixer bowl. Add the oil, juice and sugar, beating constantly. Add the whole wheat flour, wheat germ, baking powder and salt and stir until smooth. Spoon into 12 lightly greased muffin cups.

Bake in a preheated 400-degree oven for 15 to 20 minutes or until the tops are light brown. Cool in the muffin cups for 10 minutes. Invert onto a wire rack to cool completely.

MIX-AND-MATCH MUFFIN VARIATIONS

Blueberry-Cornmeal Muffins: Substitute 1 cup cornmeal for 1 cup of the whole wheat flour. Add 1 1/2 cups of fresh or frozen blueberries.

Pear-Pecan Muffins: Substitute 1 cup rye flour for 1 cup of the whole wheat flour. Add 1 pear, chopped, and 1/2 cup chopped pecans, 1/2 teaspoon cinnamon and 1/4 teaspoon nutmeg.

Apple-Oatmeal Muffins: Substitute 1 cup rolled oats for 1 cup of the whole wheat flour. Use apple juice as the liquid. Add 1 large Red Delicious apple, chopped, 1/2 cup chopped walnuts, 1/2 cup raisins, 1/2 teaspoon cinnamon, 1/4 teaspoon nutmeg and 1/4 teaspoon allspice.

Banana-Maple-Nut Muffins: Substitute 1/2 cup maple syrup for the sugar. Add 1 large ripe banana, mashed, 1/2 cup chopped walnuts and 1 teaspoon vanilla extract.

Orange-Raisin-Sunflower Muffins: Substitute 1 cup unbleached flour for 1 cup of the whole wheat flour. Use orange juice as the liquid. Add 1 tablespoon grated orange peel, 1/2 cup raisins and 1/2 cup toasted sunflower seed kernels.

ANN S. EPSTEIN—HIGH/SCOPE SENIOR RESEARCH ASSOCIATE
YPSILANTI, MICHIGAN

FOOD FOR THOUGHT

May wrap individual muffins in foil or plastic wrap and freeze for future use. Reheat in a toaster oven at 350 degrees for 10 to 15 minutes or in the microwave for 45 seconds.

YIELD: 36 SERVINGS

1 cup shortening, or 3/4 cup
  canola oil
2 cups sugar, or 1 cup sugar
  and 1 cup packed brown
  sugar
4 eggs
5 cups flour
1/2 package All-Bran cereal
2 cups 40% bran flakes
5 teaspoons baking soda
2 cups boiling water
4 cups buttermilk

S U P E R   B R A N   M U F F I N S

Cream the shortening, sugar and eggs in a large mixer bowl. Mix the flour and cereals in a bowl. Add to the creamed mixture with the baking soda, boiling water and buttermilk and beat well. Pour into a large plastic container with a tightfitting lid.

Chill, covered, overnight. Spoon the batter into greased muffin cups. Bake at 400 degrees for 18 minutes or until the muffins test done.

ERICA SAMPSON   LANSING, MICHIGAN

FOOD FOR THOUGHT

May store the batter in the refrigerator for six weeks or longer. Do not stir the batter again, but spoon off the top. To avoid raw eggs that my carry salmonella, use an equivalent amount of pasteurized egg substitute. You may also bring 2 inches of water to a boil in a small saucepan. Turn off heat. Lower the eggs carefully into the water and let stand for 1 to 1 1/2 minutes. Remove the eggs carefully. Let cool slightly before removing the shell.

*The High/Scope elementary program has a
positive effect on students' literacy skills, achievement
scores, and problem-solving abilities.*

CHILI

2 *pounds ground beef*

2 *(15-ounce) cans kidney beans*

1 *(15-ounce) can tomatoes*

1 *cup vegetable juice cocktail*

1/2 *green bell pepper, finely chopped*

3 *tablespoons chili powder*

1 *teaspoon onion salt*

1 *teaspoon salt*

1/2 *teaspoon red pepper flakes*

3 *to 4 drops of Tabasco sauce*

Brown the ground beef in a skillet, stirring until crumbly; drain. Stir in the kidney beans, tomatoes, vegetable juice cocktail, green pepper, chili powder, onion salt, salt, red pepper flakes and Tabasco sauce.

Bring to a boil and reduce heat to low. Simmer, covered, for 30 to 40 minutes, stirring occasionally.

FRIEND OF HIGH/SCOPE

Chili-for-a-Crowd

Yield: 12 servings

This recipe won first prize in the office chili cook-off. The quantities given here for chili powder and cumin will produce a middle-of-the-road flavor. If you want the chili hotter, just add more!

Brown the ground round in a Dutch oven, stirring until crumbly. Sauté the onions and green pepper in the olive oil in a skillet until the onions are translucent. Add the garlic and sauté briefly. Do not allow the garlic to brown. Add to the ground round mixture and mix well. Stir in the kidney beans, tomatoes, tomato paste, chili powder, cumin and bay leaves.

Bring to a boil and reduce heat. Simmer for 4 hours. Adjust the quantity of the chili powder and cumin by adding 3 parts chili powder to about 1 part cumin. Season with salt and pepper. Discard the bay leaves before serving.

Nancy Brickman–High/Scope Editor   Ypsilanti, Michigan

Food for Thought

Do not stint on the cooking time of this chili. It really does have to cook a long time to enhance the flavor. May cook this chili in a slow cooker all day.

- 3 pounds ground round
- 12 to 14 small yellow or white onions, chopped
- 1 medium green bell pepper, chopped
- 2 to 3 tablespoons olive oil
- 5 cloves of garlic, chopped (optional)
- 3 (16-ounce) cans deluxe dark red kidney beans
- 3 or 4 (15-ounce) cans tomatoes
- 1 (6-ounce) can tomato paste
- 2 tablespoons (or more) chili powder
- 2 teaspoons (or more) cumin
- 3 bay leaves
  Salt and pepper to taste

CINCINNATI CHILI

2 pounds lean ground beef

1 (8-ounce) can tomato sauce

1/2 cup chopped ancho chiles, or chili powder to taste

2 tablespoons cumin

1 tablespoon garlic powder, or 3 cloves of garlic, chopped

1 teaspoon cayenne

1 teaspoon sugar

1/4 teaspoon cinnamon

Salt to taste

Serve this chili with toppings such as shredded Cheddar cheese, chopped onions, sliced radishes and/or sliced black olives. It is also great served over spaghetti.

Combine the ground beef, tomato sauce, ancho chiles, cumin, garlic powder, cayenne, sugar, cinnamon and salt in a large saucepan and mix well.

Cook over medium heat for 15 minutes. Reduce heat to low. Simmer for 1 hour.

GARY TAYLOR   BLYTHEVILLE, ARKANSAS

FOOD FOR THOUGHT

Do not brown the ground beef before adding to this chili.

LENTIL CHILI

YIELD: 6 TO 8 SERVINGS

Rinse and sort the lentils. Combine the lentils, water, chick-peas, kidney beans, onion, green pepper, celery, carrot, garlic, cumin, salt and red pepper flakes in a large stockpot.

Bring to a boil and reduce heat. Simmer for 30 minutes or until the lentils are tender. Stir in the tomatoes and adjust the seasonings. Simmer until heated through.

Ladle into serving bowls. Sprinkle with the Cheddar cheese.

HIGH/SCOPE CAMP AND CONFERENCE CENTER   CLINTON, MICHIGAN

1 pound dried lentils

5 cups water

1 (16-ounce) can chick-peas, rinsed, drained

1 (16-ounce) can kidney beans, rinsed, drained

1 cup chopped onion

1/2 cup chopped green bell pepper

1/2 cup chopped celery

1/2 carrot, chopped

2 cloves of garlic, finely minced

2 teaspoons ground cumin

2 teaspoons salt

1 teaspoon red pepper flakes

1 (28-ounce) can chopped tomatoes

Shredded Cheddar cheese

YIELD: 24 SERVINGS

3 pounds ground beef

1 large onion, chopped

3 cloves of garlic, finely
    chopped

1/3 pound bacon, crisp-fried,
    crumbled

1/2 green bell pepper, chopped

12 hot tiny green peppers,
    chopped

4 pepperoncini

2 1/2 (28-ounce) cans tomatoes

1 (8-ounce) can tomato
    sauce

3 (16-ounce) cans kidney
    beans

3 tablespoons hot chili
    powder, or to taste

2 teaspoons cumin

Salt to taste

SOUTHWEST CHILI

Brown the ground beef with the onion and garlic in a large stockpot, stirring until the ground beef is crumbly; drain. Add the bacon, peppers, tomatoes, tomato sauce, undrained kidney beans, chili powder, cumin and salt.

Bring to a boil and reduce the heat. Simmer for 2 hours or longer, adding a small amount of water if needed for the desired consistency.

CLAY SHOUSE–HIGH/SCOPE DIRECTOR OF PROGRAM DEVELOPMENT
YPSILANTI, MICHIGAN

FOOD FOR THOUGHT

This spicy chili is even better served as leftovers the second or third day after preparing it.

CRAB MEAT SOUP

Sauté the green onions in the butter in a saucepan until tender. Add the celery soup, half-and-half, crab meat and crab boil and mix well.

Simmer until cooked through, stirring occasionally. Season with salt and pepper. Add enough milk to make of the desired consistency. Cook until heated through.

LAURIN HART   GRETNA, LOUISIANA

YIELD: 6 TO 8 SERVINGS

1/2 bunch green onions, chopped

1/2 cup butter

2 (10-ounce) cans cream of celery soup

2 cups half-and-half

1 pound claw crab meat, flaked

2 teaspoons liquid crab boil, or to taste

Salt and pepper

Milk

YIELD: 8 SERVINGS

1 quart oysters

7 cups fish broth

2 tablespoons butter

3 tablespoons flour

1 teaspoon lemon juice

1/2 teaspoon salt

Freshly ground black
pepper to taste

1/8 teaspoon cayenne

2 egg yolks

1/2 cup whipping cream

2 tablespoons madeira or
dry sherry

Paprika to taste

O Y S T E R   B I S Q U E

Cook the undrained oysters in a small heavy saucepan over low heat for 5 minutes or until the oysters are plump. Purée with 1 cup of the fish broth in a blender. Strain through several layers of cheesecloth into a bowl.

Melt the butter in a saucepan. Stir in the flour and the remaining fish broth. Simmer for 10 minutes. Stir in the oyster purée, lemon juice, salt, black pepper and cayenne. Add a small amount of the hot mixture to the egg yolks. Stir the egg yolks, whipping cream and wine into the hot mixture.

Cook until thickened, stirring constantly. Do not boil. Ladle into serving bowls. Sprinkle with paprika.

FRIEND OF HIGH/SCOPE

FOOD FOR THOUGHT

Since this is such a delicate soup, it should be prepared using only homemade fish broth. However, if this is not possible, use equal amounts of clam juice and water.

SHRIMP BISQUE

YIELD: 8 SERVINGS

Peel the shrimp, reserving the shells. Chop half the shrimp into small pieces. Rinse the reserved shells in cold water and place in a saucepan with the chicken broth. Bring to a boil and reduce heat. Simmer for 20 minutes. Strain the broth and discard the shells.

Sauté the onion, carrot and celery in the butter in a skillet for 3 minutes or until tender. Stir in the flour. Add the tomato paste, strained broth and whole shrimp and mix well. Simmer, covered, for 15 minutes.

Purée the shrimp mixture in batches in a blender until smooth. Strain into a saucepan. Stir in the lemon juice, wine, whipping cream, nutmeg and salt and pepper. Stir in the chopped shrimp. Cook until heated through.

FRIEND OF HIGH/SCOPE

1 pound frozen unpeeled
  small shrimp
4 cups chicken broth
1 yellow onion, chopped
1 carrot, chopped
2 ribs celery, chopped
2 tablespoons butter
6 tablespoons flour
1 teaspoon tomato paste
  Juice of $1/2$ lemon
2 tablespoons sherry
1 cup whipping cream
$1/8$ teaspoon nutmeg
  Salt and pepper to taste

YIELD: 12 SERVINGS

1 pound boneless skinless
chicken breasts

1 pound ground beef

1 pound kielbasa, cut into
1/2-inch slices

8 ounces bacon, crisp-fried,
crumbled

2 leek bulbs, rinsed, sliced

3 or 4 small turnips, peeled,
cut into small pieces

3 small zucchini, sliced

5 cloves of garlic, crushed,
or 1/2 tablespoon drained
oil-pack minced garlic

2 (14-ounce) cans clear
beef broth

1 (19-ounce) can cannellini,
rinsed

1 (19-ounce) can romano
beans, rinsed

1 (10-ounce) can niblet
corn, rinsed

1 (28-ounce) can tomatoes,
crushed

1/2 cup dry white wine

1 teaspoon marjoram

1 teaspoon parsley

1/2 teaspoon thyme

EASY CASSOULET STEW

*This stew is great to serve on a cold winter's evening with sourdough
bread and a simple lettuce salad with a vinaigrette dressing.*

Rinse the chicken and pat dry. Cut the chicken into bite-size pieces. Sauté in a nonstick skillet until tender. Brown the ground beef in a skillet, stirring until crumbly; drain. Brown the kielbasa in a nonstick skillet.

Combine the chicken, ground beef, kielbasa, bacon, leek bulbs, turnips, zucchini, garlic, beef broth, beans, corn, tomatoes, wine, marjoram, parsley and thyme in an 8-quart stockpot. Simmer for 2 hours or until the vegetables are very tender.

ANNE HUDON–HIGH/SCOPE CONFERENCE COORDINATOR AND ASSISTANT TO THE REGISTRAR
YPSILANTI, MICHIGAN

FOOD FOR THOUGHT

*A "real" cassoulet is a traditional French dish that involves white beans,
duck, lamb and other ingredients in a layered casserole. Since it also involves lots of
preparation time, I prefer to place all in one pot and let it simmer while I'm
doing something else. I have added some extra ingredients (corn for color, for example),
and have substituted meats that children prefer. Try your own variations. May chill, covered,
in the refrigerator overnight before serving to enhance the flavors.*

O V E N   B E E F   S T E W

YIELD: 6 TO 8 SERVINGS

Brown the beef in the vegetable oil in a skillet. Place the beef in a 2-quart baking dish. Combine the carrot, mushrooms, mushroom soup, wine and onion soup mix in a bowl and mix well. Pour over the beef in the prepared dish.

Bake, covered, at 350 degrees for 2½ hours, stirring occasionally.

FRIEND OF HIGH/SCOPE

FOOD FOR THOUGHT

This stew is also great served over hot cooked noodles.

2 pounds beef for stewing, cut into 1-inch cubes

2 tablespoons vegetable oil

1 medium carrot, shredded

1 (3-ounce) can chopped mushrooms, drained

1 (10-ounce) can cream of mushroom soup

⅓ cup dry red wine

2 tablespoons dry onion soup mix

CREAM OF ASPARAGUS SOUP

YIELD: 4 SERVINGS

1 pound fresh asparagus

2 tablespoons butter

1 yellow onion, finely chopped

2 tablespoons flour

4 cups chicken broth

1/2 cup whipping cream

Salt and pepper to taste

Rinse the asparagus well and drain. Trim the asparagus stems. Cut the asparagus into 2-inch pieces.

Melt the butter in a skillet. Add the onion. Sauté for 3 minutes or until the onion is translucent. Stir in the flour and chicken broth. Add the asparagus. Simmer, covered, for 20 minutes.

Purée in batches in a blender until smooth. Strain into a saucepan. Stir in the whipping cream. Cook until heated through. Season with salt and pepper.

FRIEND OF HIGH/SCOPE

B L A C K   B E A N   S O U P

YIELD: 6 SERVINGS

This recipe was given to me by a Canadian friend whom I met while living in Germany. It is great served with Mexican corn bread.

Sort and rinse the black beans. Soak in boiling water to cover in a large saucepan. Simmer for 1 hour; drain.

Fry the cumin, cumin seeds, coriander, cardamom and cinnamon in the olive oil in a large saucepan for a few minutes. Add the green chiles, onion, bacon and garlic. Fry for a few minutes or until the bacon is cooked through. Add 4 cups of the stock and the drained black beans.

Bring to a boil and reduce heat. Skim the foam off the surface. Simmer for 2 hours or until the black beans are tender, adding the remaining stock as needed. Remove enough black beans to fill a loaf pan and set aside. Process the remaining black beans in a blender until smooth and return to the saucepan. Add the whole black beans and any remaining stock. Season with salt and pepper. Ladle into soup bowls. Dollop each serving with sour cream and sprinkle with cilantro.

CHERYL PRZYGOCKI   NEW ORLEANS, LOUISIANA

FOOD FOR THOUGHT

May add a measure of rum or sherry.

1 pound dried black beans
1 tablespoon cumin
1 teaspoon cumin seeds
2 teaspoons coriander
$1/2$ teaspoon cardamom
$1/4$ teaspoon cinnamon
2 tablespoons olive oil
2 green chiles, seeded, chopped
1 onion, chopped
4 ounces bacon, chopped (optional)
2 cloves of garlic, chopped
8 cups vegetable or chicken stock
Salt and pepper to taste
Sour cream
Chopped fresh cilantro

GREEK NAVY BEAN SOUP

This recipe was the result of an "experiment."

Rinse and sort the beans. Combine with the water, carrot, onion, salt pork, olive oil and salt and pepper to taste in a large stockpot.

Bring to a boil and reduce heat. Simmer for 2 hours or until of the desired consistency.

CLAY SHOUSE-HIGH/SCOPE DIRECTOR OF PROGRAM DEVELOPMENT
YPSILANTI, MICHIGAN

YIELD: 12 TO 14 SERVINGS

2 to 3 cups dried navy beans
8 cups water
3/4 cup chopped carrot
1 medium onion, chopped
   Salt pork (optional)
3 to 5 tablespoons olive oil
   Salt and pepper

BROCCOLI SOUP

YIELD: 2 TO 4 SERVINGS

Dissolve the bouillon cubes in the hot water in a medium bowl. Sauté the onions in a large nonstick saucepan over medium heat until tender. Add the broccoli, potatoes and bouillon.

Bring to a boil and reduce heat. Simmer for 45 minutes. Stir in the hot White Sauce. Sprinkle with the Parmesan cheese.

WHITE SAUCE

6 tablespoons margarine

6 tablespoons flour

2 cups milk

Heat the margarine in a saucepan over low heat until melted. Blend in the flour. Cook over low heat until smooth and bubbly, stirring constantly. Remove from heat.

Stir in the milk. Bring to a boil, stirring constantly. Boil for 1 minute or until thickened, stirring constantly.

TINA EVERARD   YPSILANTI, MICHIGAN

4 chicken bouillon cubes

2 cups hot water

2 small onions, chopped

2 heads broccoli, chopped

4 medium potatoes, chopped
    White Sauce

1 to 2 tablespoons grated
    Parmesan cheese

YIELD: 6 SERVINGS

GAZPACHO

1 cup coarsely chopped
tomatoes

$^{1}/_{2}$ cup chopped green bell
pepper

$^{1}/_{2}$ cup chopped celery

$^{1}/_{2}$ cup chopped seeded
cucumber

$^{1}/_{2}$ cup chopped onion

2 teaspoons chopped parsley

1 teaspoon chopped chives
Minced cloves of garlic to
taste

3 tablespoons tarragon wine
vinegar

2 tablespoons olive oil

1 teaspoon salt

$^{1}/_{4}$ teaspoon pepper

$^{1}/_{2}$ teaspoon Worcestershire
sauce (optional)

2 cups tomato juice or spicy
vegetable juice cocktail

Combine the tomatoes, green pepper, celery, cucumber, onion, parsley, chives, garlic, vinegar, olive oil, salt, pepper, Worcestershire sauce and tomato juice in a large glass bowl and mix well.

Chill, covered, for at least 4 hours.

CAROL HOFFER   ANN ARBOR, MICHIGAN

FOOD FOR THOUGHT

This recipe is easy to make in large batches and is a great use for summer tomatoes. Serve from plastic tumblers at summer lawn parties with separate bowls of garnishes such as chopped onion, chopped cucumber, bread croutons and plain yogurt for guests to use as desired. May store in the refrigerator for up to 1 week.

Split Pea, Lentil and Barley Soup

Rinse and sort the split peas and lentils. Dissolve the bouillon cubes in the boiling water in a bowl.

Combine the split peas, lentils, bouillon and barley in a large stockpot. Bring to a boil and reduce heat. Simmer for 45 minutes or until the split peas and lentils are tender. Add the celery, carrot, onion, garlic and pepper. Simmer for 45 minutes. Add additional water if needed for the desired consistency. Adjust the seasonings.

HIGH/SCOPE CAMP AND CONFERENCE CENTER   CLINTON, MICHIGAN

YIELD: 4 TO 6 SERVINGS

1 cup dried green split peas
1/2 cup dried yellow split peas
1/2 cup dried lentils
2 chicken bouillon cubes
8 cups boiling water
1/2 cup barley
1 cup chopped celery
1 cup chopped or shredded carrot
1 large onion, chopped
1 clove of garlic, minced
1/4 teaspoon pepper

Good Cheap Soup

YIELD: 4 TO 6 SERVINGS

4 (10-ounce) cans vegetable broth

¹/₄ cup (about) acini di pepe

1 (16-ounce) package frozen stir-fry vegetables

Chopped cilantro to taste

Garlic powder to taste

Salt and pepper to taste

10 mushrooms, quartered

I came across this recipe while surfing the Internet.

Bring the broth to a boil in a large saucepan. Stir in the pasta. Cook for 5 minutes. Add the vegetables, cilantro, garlic powder and salt and pepper to taste. Simmer for 15 minutes. Add the mushrooms. Simmer for 10 minutes.

CHERYL BOGLARSKY   BELLEVILLE, MICHIGAN

S T U F F E D   B E L L   P E P P E R S

YIELD: 8 SERVINGS

Cut the tops off the green peppers and remove the seeds. Bring the green pepper shells to a boil in water to cover in a large saucepan. Boil for 5 minutes; drain.

Brown the ground beef with the onion in a skillet, stirring until the ground beef is crumbly; drain. Add the tomatoes, corn and salt and pepper. Spoon into the green pepper shells. Sprinkle with bread crumbs.

Place each stuffed green pepper in a greased muffin cup containing 1 tablespoon hot water. Bake at 325 degrees for 1 hour.

FRIEND OF HIGH/SCOPE

8 green bell peppers

1 pound ground beef

1 small onion, chopped

2 cups chopped tomatoes

1 1/2 cups drained whole kernel corn

Salt and pepper to taste

1/4 cup bread crumbs

SPAGHETTI SAUCE

YIELD: 4 TO 6 SERVINGS

1 pound ground beef

1 onion, chopped

1/2 green bell pepper, chopped

1 teaspoon bacon drippings

1 tablespoon shortening

1/2 cup water

1/2 cup catsup

1/2 cup chili sauce

1 tablespoon Heinz 57 sauce

1 teaspoon Worcestershire
   sauce

1 cup canned tomatoes

Salt and pepper to taste

Brown the ground beef with the onion and green pepper in the bacon drippings, shortening and water in a large skillet, stirring until the ground beef is crumbly; drain. Add the catsup, chili sauce, Heinz 57 sauce, Worcestershire sauce, tomatoes and salt and pepper and mix well.

Cook the sauce over low heat for 1 hour, stirring occasionally. Serve over hot cooked spaghetti.

FRIEND OF HIGH/SCOPE

LASAGNA

YIELD: 6 TO 8 SERVINGS

Brown the ground beef in a skillet, stirring until crumbly; drain. Add the tomatoes, tomato sauce, tomato paste, tomato soup, oregano, basil, garlic powder, salt, pepper, rosemary and lasagna sauce mix and mix well.

Alternate layers of the ground beef sauce, noodles, ricotta cheese, mozzarella cheese and Parmesan cheese in a greased 9x13-inch baking dish, ending with the Parmesan cheese. Bake at 350 degrees for 30 to 45 minutes or until heated through.

FRIEND OF HIGH/SCOPE

1½ pounds ground beef

1 (15-ounce) can tomatoes, drained

1 (15-ounce) can tomato sauce

1 (6-ounce) can tomato paste

1 (10-ounce) can tomato soup

2 teaspoons oregano

1½ teaspoons basil

1 teaspoon garlic powder

1 teaspoon salt

1 teaspoon pepper

½ teaspoon rosemary

1 envelope lasagna sauce mix

8 lasagna noodles, cooked, drained

Ricotta or cottage cheese to taste

Mozzarella cheese to taste

Grated Parmesan cheese to taste

YIELD: 6 TO 8 SERVINGS

2 *medium onions, chopped*

3 *tablespoons olive oil*

2 *cups tomato sauce*

2 *teaspoons oregano*

1 *teaspoon basil*

1/4 *cup chopped parsley*

 Salt to taste

1 *(4-ounce) can mushrooms, drained*

3/4 *cup drained red kidney beans*

8 *ounces lasagna noodles*

2 *cups ricotta or small curd cottage cheese*

1 *pound mozzarella cheese, shredded*

1/2 *cup grated Parmesan cheese*

VEGETARIAN LASAGNA

Sauté the onions in the olive oil in a skillet until tender. Stir in the tomato sauce, oregano, basil, parsley and salt. Cook for 30 minutes or until thickened, stirring occasionally. Stir in the mushrooms and kidney beans.

Cook the lasagna noodles in boiling water to cover in a saucepan until tender; drain. Rinse the lasagna noodles in cold water.

Layer the lasagna noodles, sauce, ricotta cheese, mozzarella cheese and Parmesan cheese 1/3 at a time in a greased 9x13-inch baking dish. Bake, covered, at 375 degrees for 15 minutes. Bake, uncovered, for 5 minutes longer.

HIGH/SCOPE CAMP AND CONFERENCE CENTER   CLINTON, MICHIGAN

CHICKEN ROTELLE

YIELD: 30 SERVINGS

Combine the tomato sauce and sugar in a large saucepan. Stir in the salt, pepper, Parmesan cheese and Romano cheese and garlic mix. Cook until heated through.

Cook the pasta in boiling water in a saucepan until tender; drain. Layer in a large serving dish. Brown the ground chicken in a large nonstick skillet, stirring until crumbly; drain. Layer over the pasta.

Stir the mozzarella cheese and cottage cheese into the tomato sauce mixture. Heat for 5 minutes or until the cheeses are melted, stirring constantly. Pour into the prepared dish. Serve immediately.

KASENA DAILEY   BEAVERTON, OREGON

1 (No. 10) can tomato sauce (106 ounces or 13 cups)

1/4 cup sugar

1/8 teaspoon salt

1/8 teaspoon pepper

1/2 cup grated Parmesan cheese

1/4 cup grated Romano cheese and garlic mix

5 pounds rotelle

5 pounds ground chicken

2 pounds shredded mozzarella cheese

2 pounds cottage cheese

79

YIELD: 6 SERVINGS

1 (2-ounce) jar dried
   chipped beef
6 skinned chicken breast
   halves
6 slices bacon
1 (10-ounce) can cream of
   mushroom soup
1 cup sour cream

BAKED CHICKEN

Rinse the chipped beef in cold water; drain. Arrange in a greased 8x12-inch baking dish. Rinse the chicken and pat dry. Arrange over the chipped beef. Place a slice of bacon on each piece of chicken.

Bake in a preheated 350-degree oven for 30 minutes. Pour a mixture of the mushroom soup and sour cream over the chicken. Bake for 25 minutes or until the chicken is cooked through.

FRIEND OF HIGH/SCOPE

CHICKEN CASSEROLE

YIELD: 8 SERVINGS

Rinse the chicken. Cook the chicken in water to cover in a saucepan until cooked through. Drain, reserving 2 cups chicken broth. Arrange the cooked chicken in a greased 8-inch baking dish.

Pour a mixture of the chicken soup and evaporated milk over the chicken. Mix the stuffing mix with the reserved chicken broth in a bowl. Spread over the top of the chicken. Bake at 350 degrees for 30 minutes or until heated through.

BETSY AND CALLIE COLE   MONROE, MICHIGAN

1¹⁄₂ to 2 pounds boneless chicken breast halves

1 (10-ounce) can cream of chicken soup

¹⁄₂ (12-ounce) can evaporated milk

1 (6-ounce) package Stove Top chicken stuffing mix

YIELD: 4 SERVINGS

4 skinless boneless chicken breasts

1 large onion

1 clove of garlic

1/4 cup curry powder

3 tablespoons paprika

1/2 stick cinnamon

1 bay leaf

Grandma's Foolproof Rice

CHICKEN CURRY

In its original form, this recipe was made by my grandmother for my grandfather. Grandfather worked as an assembly-line worker at Ford Motor Company for many years. Because he sometimes worked an extra shift, Grandmother would make this meal so Grandfather could eat dinner at his leisure. Over the years, this low-fat version evolved. The original recipe called for whole fryer pieces sautéed in vegetable oil. Either way, this recipe is a family favorite.

Rinse the chicken and pat dry. Cut the chicken into 2-inch pieces. Spray a 4-quart saucepan with nonstick cooking spray. Add the onion and garlic. Sauté over moderate heat until tender. Add the chicken pieces, curry powder, paprika, cinnamon stick and bay leaf.

Sauté until the chicken is coated with the spices, adding additional nonstick cooking spray if needed. Add enough water to cover the chicken. Simmer, covered, for 25 minutes or until the chicken is cooked through and a rich broth remains. Discard the cinnamon stick and bay leaf. Serve over Grandma's Foolproof Rice.

GRANDMA'S FOOLPROOF RICE

4 cups water

2 1/2 cups white rice

Bring the water to a boil in a small ovenproof saucepan. Add the rice. Boil, uncovered, for 10 minutes; drain.

Bake, covered, in a preheated 350-degree oven for 10 minutes.

GAVIN HAQUE–HIGH/SCOPE TRAINING COORDINATOR   YPSILANTI, MICHIGAN

CURRIED CHICKEN

YIELD: 4 SERVINGS

Rinse the chicken and pat dry. Arrange the chicken in a baking dish. Mix the marmalade with enough of the water in a bowl to form a medium consistency. Stir in the curry powder. Pour over the chicken.

Bake, covered, at 350 degrees for 30 minutes. Turn over the chicken. Bake, covered, for 10 minutes. Bake, uncovered, for 10 minutes longer, basting or turning frequently.

FRIEND OF HIGH/SCOPE

FOOD FOR THOUGHT

May use your favorite chicken pieces in this recipe.

4 *chicken breast halves*

1/2 *to* 3/4 *(16-ounce) jar low-sugar marmalade*

1/4 *to* 1/2 *cup water*

1/2 *teaspoon curry powder*

HAWAIIAN CHICKEN

YIELD: 4 SERVINGS

2 pounds chicken pieces
  Salt and pepper to taste
1 (8-ounce) can sliced
  pineapple
2 tablespoons honey
1/3 cup Heinz 57 sauce

Rinse the chicken and pat dry. Place in a nonstick 8x12-inch baking dish. Season with salt and pepper. Bake at 400 degrees for 30 minutes.

Drain the pineapple, reserving 2 tablespoons of the juice. Mix the reserved pineapple juice, honey and Heinz 57 sauce in a bowl. Pour over the chicken.

Bake for 25 minutes or until the chicken is cooked through, basting occasionally. Arrange the pineapple over the chicken. Bake for 10 minutes. Drain any excess grease from the sauce and serve over the chicken.

FRIEND OF HIGH/SCOPE

CHICKEN À LA ORANGE

YIELD: 4 SERVINGS

Rinse the chicken and pat dry. Sauté the chicken in the butter in a skillet for 4 to 5 minutes or until the chicken is cooked through. Remove with a slotted spoon and set aside. Mix the cornstarch and orange juice in a bowl. Stir in the Heinz 57 sauce and orange marmalade. Pour into the skillet.

Cook until thickened, stirring constantly. Return the chicken to the skillet. Cook until heated through. Garnish each serving with slivered almonds.

FRIEND OF HIGH/SCOPE

1 pound chicken breast
  fillets or thighs
2 tablespoons butter
2 teaspoons cornstarch
2/3 cup orange juice
1/3 cup Heinz 57 sauce
1/4 cup orange marmalade
  Toasted slivered almonds

YIELD: 6 TO 8 SERVINGS

6 to 8 chicken breasts

1 (10-ounce) can tomato
soup

1 (10-ounce) can golden
mushroom soup

1 small jar pearl onions

1 clove of garlic, minced

1 (16-ounce) package egg
noodles

Butter to taste

Poppy seeds to taste

CHICKEN BREASTS
À LA MARENGO

Rinse the chicken and pat dry. Brown the chicken in a small amount of vegetable oil in a skillet. Add the tomato soup, golden mushroom soup, onions and garlic. Bring to a boil and reduce heat. Simmer for 35 to 45 minutes or until the chicken is tender and cooked through.

Cook the egg noodles in a saucepan using the package directions; drain. Add the butter and toss until the noodles are coated. Sprinkle with the poppy seeds. Serve the chicken with or over the poppy seed noodles.

NANCY L. HEYWOOD–HIGH/SCOPE HUMAN RESOURCES REPRESENTATIVE
YPSILANTI, MICHIGAN

FOOD FOR THOUGHT

For variety, use pork chops instead of chicken in this recipe.

CHICKEN WITH SPICY PEANUT SAUCE

This is a lightly sauced dish.

Rinse the chicken and pat dry. Cut the chicken into bite-size pieces. Stir-fry the chicken in a small amount of vegetable oil and ginger in a skillet until cooked through.

Combine the peanut butter and 5 tablespoons vegetable oil in a saucepan and mix well. Stir in the soy sauce, sugar, vinegar, cayenne and green onions. Bring to a boil and reduce heat. Simmer for 10 minutes. Stir in the cooked chicken. Spoon over the hot cooked noodles.

HIGH/SCOPE CAMP AND CONFERENCE CENTER   CLINTON, MICHIGAN

1½ pounds chicken breast fillets
1 teaspoon ginger
3 tablespoons peanut butter
5 tablespoons vegetable oil
¼ cup soy sauce
¼ cup sugar
4 teaspoons white vinegar
½ teaspoon cayenne
2 to 4 green onions, minced
12 ounces noodles, cooked

FOOD FOR THOUGHT

May substitute half the vegetable oil for sesame oil in the sauce.

S U N B U R S T   S T I R - F R Y

YIELD: 4 SERVINGS

1 (20-ounce) can pineapple
  chunks

1/3 cup soy sauce

1 tablespoon cornstarch

1 tablespoon sesame oil

1 large chicken breast

2 tablespoons vegetable oil

1/2 teaspoon ginger

2 cloves of garlic, minced

2 carrots, sliced

1 green bell pepper,
  julienned

3 green onions, chopped

Hot cooked rice

Drain the pineapple, reserving 1/3 cup juice. Combine the reserved pineapple juice, soy sauce, cornstarch and sesame oil in a saucepan and mix well. Cook until thickened, stirring constantly.

Rinse the chicken and pat dry. Debone and skin the chicken. Cut the chicken into pieces. Stir-fry the chicken in the vegetable oil in a skillet for 2 minutes. Stir in the ginger and garlic. Add the pineapple, carrots and green pepper. Steam, covered, for 2 to 3 minutes or until the vegetables are tender-crisp. Add the sauce and green onions. Stir-fry until heated through. Spoon over the hot cooked rice.

HIGH/SCOPE CAMP AND CONFERENCE CENTER   CLINTON, MICHIGAN

Teriyaki Chicken

YIELD: 4 SERVINGS

Rinse the chicken and pat dry. Cut the chicken into slices. Arrange in a 9x13-inch baking dish sprayed with nonstick cooking spray.

Combine the sugar, soy sauce, vegetable oil, mustard, honey and garlic in a small bowl and mix well. Pour over the chicken. Marinate, covered, in the refrigerator for 1 hour.

Bake, uncovered, at 350 degrees for 25 to 30 minutes or until the chicken is cooked through. Serve over the hot cooked rice.

High/Scope Camp and Conference Center   Clinton, Michigan

3 pounds boneless chicken breasts
1 cup sugar
1/2 cup soy sauce
1/4 cup vegetable oil
3 tablespoons dry mustard
3 tablespoons honey
6 cloves of garlic, minced
Hot cooked white rice

CHICKEN IN WINE SAUCE

YIELD: 2 TO 4 SERVINGS

2 large chicken breasts, split

1 1/2 tablespoons flour

1/2 teaspoon salt

1/4 teaspoon pepper

4 tablepoons margarine

8 ounces mushrooms, thinly sliced

1/4 cup chopped onion

1/4 cup chopped parsley

1 cup wine

2 cups hot cooked rice

Rinse the chicken and pat dry. Debone and skin the chicken. Combine the flour, salt and pepper in a plastic food storage bag. Add the chicken and shake to coat well.

Melt 2 tablespoons of the margarine in a large skillet over medium heat. Add the chicken, reserving the flour mixture. Cook the chicken until brown and remove from the skillet. Add the remaining 2 tablespoons margarine, mushrooms, onion and 2 tablespoons of the parsley to the skillet. Sauté until the onion is transparent. Remove from the heat.

Stir in the reserved flour mixture. Blend in the wine. Bring to a boil, stirring frequently. Add the chicken. Cover and reduce heat. Simmer for 25 minutes or until the chicken is tender and cooked through. Serve over the hot cooked rice. Sprinkle with the remaining 2 tablespoons parsley.

EMILY KOEPP-HIGH/SCOPE DIRECTOR OF MARKETING AND FUND DEVELOPMENT
YPSILANTI, MICHIGAN

Chicken Salad Casserole

Yield: 8 servings

A great dish to take to potluck dinners.

Combine the chicken, celery, almonds, onion and salt in a large bowl and mix well. Stir in the mayonnaise, sour cream and lemon juice. Spoon into a greased 9x13-inch baking dish. Sprinkle with the cheese and potato chips.

Bake at 450 degrees for 20 to 25 minutes.

Jan Gifford–High/Scope Elementary Division Secretary
Ypsilanti, Michigan

- 2 cups chopped cooked chicken
- 2 cups chopped celery
- 1/2 cup chopped blanched almonds
- 2 tablespoons grated onion
- 1/2 teaspoon salt
- 1/2 cup mayonnaise
- 3/4 cup sour cream
- 2 tablespoons lemon juice
- 1/2 cup shredded sharp Cheddar cheese
- 1 cup crushed potato chips

YIELD: 4 TO 6 SERVINGS

1/4 cup chopped celery

1/4 cup chopped onion

3 tablespoons margarine

2 (6-ounce) cans
  mushrooms, drained

1 (2-ounce) jar pimento,
  drained

4 cups chopped cooked
  turkey or chicken

2 cups sour cream

2 (10-ounce) cans cream of
  mushroom soup

16 ounces spaghetti, cooked
  Parmesan cheese to taste

TURKEY TETRAZZINI

Sauté the celery and onion in the margarine in a small skillet until tender. Combine the sautéed vegetables, mushrooms, pimento, turkey, sour cream and mushroom soup in a large bowl. Stir in the spaghetti. Add a small amount of water if needed for the desired consistency. Spoon into a large baking dish. Sprinkle with the Parmesan cheese.

Bake at 350 degrees for 40 minutes or until bubbly.

HIGH/SCOPE CAMP AND CONFERENCE CENTER   CLINTON, MICHIGAN

BROILED GARLIC HALIBUT

YIELD: 2 SERVINGS

Combine the garlic, olive oil, basil, lemon juice, salt and pepper in a glass dish. Add the halibut. Marinate, covered, in the refrigerator for 2 hours. Drain the halibut, reserving the marinade. Place the halibut on an oiled rack in a broiler pan.

Broil 4 inches from the heat source for 5 minutes on each side, basting with the reserved marinade. Sprinkle with the parsley just before serving.

MARGY SHOUSE   YPSILANTI, MICHIGAN

1 large or 2 small cloves of garlic, chopped

6 tablespoons olive oil

1 teaspoon dried basil

1 tablespoon lemon or lime juice

1 1/2 teaspoons salt

1 teaspoon freshly ground pepper

2 halibut steaks, 1 inch thick

Chopped parsley to taste

Barbecued Shrimp

YIELD: 4 TO 5 SERVINGS

1 cup olive oil

1 tablespoon plus
  1 teaspoon salt

2 teaspoons ground pepper

2 teaspoons crushed fresh
  oregano leaves

2 teaspoons crushed fresh
  rosemary leaves

3 bay leaves

25 cloves of unpeeled garlic,
  mashed

2 pounds large whole shrimp

1 cup dry white wine

Mix the olive oil, salt, pepper, oregano, rosemary, bay leaves and garlic in a large skillet. Add the shrimp. Cook over medium-high heat for 15 to 20 minutes or until the shrimp turn pink and the liquid has almost evaporated, stirring occasionally.

Reduce heat to low. Add the wine. Simmer for 5 to 7 minutes or until the liquid is reduced by half. Remove the bay leaves before serving.

JANIS DERING   CHALMETTE, LOUISIANA

NORTHWEST CIOPPINO

YIELD: 4 SERVINGS

This recipe came from the now-closed Sweetwater Restaurant in Redmond, Washington.

Core the tomatoes and cut into halves. Place the tomatoes and water in a 2-quart saucepan. Bring to a boil and reduce heat. Simmer, covered, until thickened and of a sauce consistency, stirring constantly.

Sauté 1/2 of the garlic and the onion in 1/2 of the olive oil in a skillet until the onion is transparent. Add the tomato mixture and herbs. Simmer for 30 minutes or until reduced to 2/3. Add the sugar, red wine vinegar, honey and salt and pepper. Return to a boil and remove from heat.

Sauté the remaining garlic in the remaining olive oil in a 4-quart saucepan. Add the clams, crab and marinara sauce. Simmer until the clams have opened. Discard any clams that do not open. Add the scallops, prawns, cod and salmon. Return to a simmer. Turn off the heat. Let stand, covered, for 3 to 5 minutes. Serve immediately.

BONNIE NEUGEBAUER   REDMOND, WASHINGTON

4 tomatoes

2/3 cup water

6 cloves of garlic, crushed

1 white onion, finely chopped

1/4 cup olive oil

1 tablespoon each chopped fresh basil, oregano, thyme, marjoram and parsley

1 tablespoon sugar

1 tablespoon red wine vinegar

1/4 cup honey

Salt and pepper to taste

1 pound clams and/or mussels, cleaned

1 (2-pound) Dungeness crab, steamed, cracked, cleaned

4 ounces sea scallops

12 (16- to 20-count) black tiger prawns

8 ounces ling cod

1/2 king salmon fillet

YIELD: 4 SERVINGS

4 egg whites

2 tablespoons water

1 teaspoon sugar

1/4 teaspoon salt

4 egg yolks

2 tablespoons flour

6 tablespoons water

1/8 teaspoon pepper

Shortening for frying

Confectioners' sugar

AUNT ANNA'S OMELET

*My great-aunt, born at the close of the Civil War, prepared and sent this
omelet to new mothers during their recovery from childbirth.*

Beat the egg whites in a mixer bowl until frothy. Add the 2 tablespoons water, sugar and
salt, beating constantly until stiff but not dry. Beat the egg yolks lightly in a bowl. Add
the flour, 6 tablespoons water and pepper and mix well.

Heat enough shortening in a large skillet to cover the bottom of the skillet. Pour
in the egg yolk mixture. Layer the meringue over the top. Cook, covered, over low heat
for 6 to 8 minutes or until a knife inserted near the center comes out clean. Fold the
omelet over. Serve immediately with confectioners' sugar.

MARLENE BARR   YPSILANTI, MICHIGAN

P A S T A   P R I M A V E R A

Cook the broccoli in a small amount of water in a saucepan until tender-crisp. Drain and set aside. Cook the mushrooms, onion and carrot in the olive oil in a large skillet until golden and tender-crisp. Add the red pepper. Cook until tender.

Mix the evaporated milk, instant bouillon, cornstarch and salt with a fork in a 2-cup measure. Stir into the vegetable mixture. Bring to a boil. Boil for 1 minute or until clear. Stir in the tomato, Parmesan cheese, parsley and broccoli. Add the spaghetti and toss to coat well. Cook until heated through. Serve immediately.

HIGH/SCOPE CAMP AND CONFERENCE CENTER   CLINTON, MICHIGAN

1/2 small bunch broccoli, cut into 1-inch pieces (2 cups)

12 ounces fresh mushrooms, cut into halves

1 small onion, minced

1 small carrot, cut into thin strips

2 tablespoons olive oil

1 small red bell pepper, cut into thin strips

1 (12-ounce) can evaporated skim milk

2 teaspoons instant chicken bouillon

1 1/4 teaspoons cornstarch

1/2 teaspoon salt

1 medium tomato, seeded, chopped

2 tablespoons grated Parmesan cheese

2 tablespoons minced parsley

12 ounces spaghetti or linguini, cooked

YIELD: 1 TO 1½ CUPS

1 (12-ounce) can tomato
  paste
¼ cup chopped parsley
2 tablespoons Italian
  seasonings
1 tablespoon sugar
2 teaspoons oregano
2 teaspoons basil
½ teaspoon thyme
½ teaspoon rosemary
2 cloves of garlic, minced
½ teaspoon salt
½ teaspoon black pepper
½ teaspoon cumin
¼ teaspoon red pepper flakes

Pizza Sauce

Combine the tomato paste, parsley, Italian seasonings, sugar, oregano, basil, thyme, rosemary, garlic, salt, black pepper, cumin and red pepper flakes in a bowl and mix well.

High/Scope Camp and Conference Center   Clinton, Michigan

Food for Thought

*Spread this special pizza sauce over your favorite pizza dough and
add your own variations for toppings.*

The Incredible Crustless Quiche

Yield: 8 servings

This is the easiest way to make a quiche. It is much easier than making a French pastry crust. Serve warm or at room temperature with a salad and steamed broccoli or asparagus.

Mix the cheese, bacon, mushrooms, onion, thyme, oregano and pepper in a large bowl. Spread evenly in a greased 12-inch porcelain or stoneware quiche dish. Whisk the eggs and whipping cream in a bowl. Pour into the prepared quiche dish.

Bake at 325 or 350 degrees for 30 to 45 minutes or until the quiche is set and puffed up and the top is brown. Let stand for 5 to 10 minutes before serving.

Anne Hudon—High/Scope Conference Coordinator and Assistant to the Registrar
Ypsilanti, Michigan

Food for Thought

May need to reduce the oven temperature while baking if the top is becoming too brown before the quiche is set.

8 to 12 ounces Gruyère cheese

Crumbled crisp-fried bacon to taste

1/2 cup sliced mushrooms

1 small onion, chopped

1/4 teaspoon thyme

1/2 teaspoon oregano

Freshly ground pepper to taste

4 eggs

2/3 cup whipping cream

YIELD: 6 SERVINGS

1 cup milk

3 eggs

2 cups shredded mozzarella cheese, Swiss cheese or Cheddar cheese

1/8 teaspoon salt

1/8 teaspoon cayenne

1/8 teaspoon nutmeg

1 (12-ounce) package bacon, crisp-fried, crumbled

1 (8-ounce) package frozen broccoli spears, thawed, drained

Chopped red bell pepper to taste

Chopped green onions to taste

1 (8-inch) pie shell

BROCCOLI QUICHE

Process the milk, eggs, mozzarella cheese, salt, cayenne and nutmeg in a blender until blended. Add the bacon, broccoli, red pepper and green onions. Blend until of the desired consistency. Pour into the pie shell.

Bake at 375 degrees for 45 minutes or until the center is set. Cool slightly before serving.

JAN GIFFORD—HIGH/SCOPE ELEMENTARY DIVISION SECRETARY
YPSILANTI, MICHIGAN

HELLZAPOPPIN CHEESE RICE

I first tested this easy recipe on my husband when we were newlyweds.
It is great served as a main dish or as a side dish.

Cook the spinach in a saucepan using the package directions; drain. Beat the eggs in a mixer bowl until light. Add the milk, onion, Worcestershire sauce and seasonings. Fold in the cheese, spinach and rice. Pour into a greased medium-size casserole. Pour the melted butter over the top.

Bake at 375 degrees for 35 minutes.

BARBARA HERTZ WALLGREN   YPSILANTI, MICHIGAN

1 (10-ounce) package frozen chopped spinach

4 eggs

1 cup milk

2 tablespoons minced onion

1 tablespoon Worcestershire sauce

2 teaspoons salt

1/8 teaspoon thyme

1/8 teaspoon marjoram

1 pound sharp Cheddar cheese, grated

4 cups cooked rice

1/4 cup melted butter

YIELD: 8 SERVINGS

1/4 cup margarine
1 medium onion, chopped
2 cups rice
4 cups chicken stock
1/4 cup chopped parsley
1/2 teaspoon marjoram
1/4 teaspoon thyme

RICE PILAF

Melt the margarine in a skillet. Add the onion. Sauté for 2 minutes. Add the uncooked rice. Sauté for 2 minutes or until the rice is coated with the margarine.

Mix the chicken stock, parsley, marjoram and thyme in a bowl. Add to the rice mixture and mix well. Spoon into a 2-quart baking dish sprayed with nonstick cooking spray. Bake, covered, at 350 degrees for 40 minutes or until the stock has been absorbed.

HIGH/SCOPE CAMP AND CONFERENCE CENTER   CLINTON, MICHIGAN

GRANDMA'S BAKED BEANS

YIELD: 12 SERVINGS

My mother compiled this recipe from watching her mother-in-law's preparations. My grandmother didn't use a recipe, but baked by adding "a little of this" and "more of that."

Rinse and sort the beans. Soak the beans in water to cover in a large saucepan overnight. Add the baking soda. Bring to a boil. Boil for 20 to 30 minutes or until the beans are tender. Drain and rinse the beans.

Place the onion in the center of a 2- to 3-quart baking dish. Add the beans. Combine 2 cups water, brown sugar, molasses, salt and dry mustard in a bowl. Pour over the beans. Cover the top with bacon slices.

Bake at 325 degrees for 2 hours or until the beans are light brown and tender, turning the bacon to brown on both sides and covering loosely with foil when the bacon is brown.

MARLENE BARR   YPSILANTI, MICHIGAN

3 cups dried navy beans
1½ teaspoons baking soda
1 small onion
2 cups water
5 tablespoons brown sugar
5 tablespoons molasses
1 teaspoon salt
1 teaspoon dry mustard
Bacon slices

YIELD: 8 SERVINGS

1 (10-ounce) package frozen
  chopped broccoli
1/2 cup chopped onion
2 tablespoons butter
2 cups brown rice
2 eggs, lightly beaten
2 cups milk
1 teaspoon salt
1/4 teaspoon pepper
1 1/2 cups shredded sharp
  Cheddar cheese

BROCCOLI AND CHEESE CASSEROLE

Cook the broccoli in a saucepan using the package directions until tender-crisp. Drain and set aside. Sauté the onion in the butter in a skillet until the onion is transparent. Add the uncooked rice. Sauté for a few minutes.

Combine the eggs, milk, salt and pepper in a large bowl and mix well. Stir in the cheese, broccoli and sautéed rice mixture. Spoon into a buttered baking dish. Bake at 325 degrees for 1 hour or until bubbly.

HIGH/SCOPE CAMP AND CONFERENCE CENTER   CLINTON, MICHIGAN

FOOD FOR THOUGHT

May use fresh broccoli in this recipe.

SUMMER SQUASH AND CORN CASSEROLE

YIELD: 10 SERVINGS

Cook the squash in a small amount of water in a saucepan until tender; drain. Sauté the onion and green pepper in 2 tablespoons margarine in a skillet until tender.

Combine the squash, green pepper mixture, corn, egg and seasoned salt in a large bowl and mix well. Stir in the cheese and 1/2 of the stuffing mix. Spoon into a nonstick 9-inch baking dish.

Bake at 350 degrees for 20 minutes. Sprinkle with a mixture of the remaining stuffing mix and 1 tablespoon margarine. Bake for 10 minutes.

MARILYN E. THOMAS–HIGH/SCOPE BOARD OF DIRECTORS   YELLOW SPRINGS, OHIO

- 1 pound yellow squash or zucchini, sliced
- 1 large onion, chopped
- 1 small green bell pepper, chopped
- 2 tablespoons margarine
- 2 (16-ounce) cans cream-style corn
- 1 egg, beaten
- 1 teaspoon seasoned salt
- 1 cup shredded Cheddar cheese
- 1 1/2 cups Stove Top corn bread stuffing mix
- 1 tablespoon melted margarine

JIFFY CORN CASSEROLE

YIELD: 6 TO 8 SERVINGS

1 (8-ounce) can cream-style corn

1 (8-ounce) can whole kernel corn

1/2 cup vegetable oil

1 cup sour cream

2 eggs

1/2 cup sugar

1 (9-ounce) package corn muffin mix

Combine the cream-style corn, undrained whole kernel corn, vegetable oil, sour cream, eggs, sugar and corn muffin mix in a large bowl and mix well. Pour into a greased 8x11-inch baking dish.

Bake at 350 degrees for 35 minutes or until golden brown.

TINA EVERARD   YPSILANTI, MICHIGAN

BAKED CHEESE GRITS

YIELD: 6 SERVINGS

Bring the water to a boil in a saucepan over high heat. Add the salt and grits, stirring constantly. Reduce heat to low. Cook for 5 minutes or until thickened, stirring occasionally. Remove from heat. Stir in the flour, margarine, cheese, Worcestershire sauce and paprika.

Beat the eggs in a small bowl. Stir a small amount of the hot grits into the eggs; stir the eggs into the hot grits. Pour into a greased 1¹/₂-quart baking dish. Bake, uncovered, at 350 degrees for 30 to 40 minutes or until firm.

MARILYN E. THOMAS—HIGH/SCOPE BOARD OF DIRECTORS   YELLOW SPRINGS, OHIO

4 cups water

¹/₂ teaspoon salt

1 cup quick-cooking grits

1 tablespoon flour

1 tablespoon margarine

3 cups shredded Cheddar cheese

1 tablespoon Worcestershire sauce

2 teaspoons paprika

2 eggs

1 cup chopped onion

1 (10-ounce) can cream of
   mushroom or cream of
   chicken soup

2 cups sour cream

1/2 cup melted butter

2 pounds frozen southern-
   style potato cubes

2 cups shredded sharp
   Cheddar cheese

Crumbled potato chips

POTATO CASSEROLE

Combine the onion, cream of mushroom soup, sour cream and butter in a large bowl and mix well. Stir in the potatoes. Spread in a nonstick 9x13-inch baking dish. Sprinkle with the cheese and potato chips.

Bake at 375 degrees for 1 hour.

FRIEND OF HIGH/SCOPE

TEXAS POTATOES

YIELD: 6 SERVINGS

Sauté the onion in the margarine in a skillet. Combine the sautéed onion, cheese, sour cream, soup and potatoes in a large bowl and mix well. Spoon into a baking dish sprayed with nonstick cooking spray. Sprinkle with cornflakes.

Bake, covered, at 350 degrees for 30 minutes. Bake, uncovered, for 15 minutes longer or just until the potatoes are tender.

HIGH/SCOPE CAMP AND CONFERENCE CENTER   CLINTON, MICHIGAN

$1/2$ cup chopped onion or green onion

$1/4$ cup margarine

2 cups shredded sharp Cheddar cheese

1 cup sour cream

1 (10-ounce) can cream of chicken soup

2 pounds potatoes, peeled, chopped
Cornflakes

YIELD: 1 SERVING

1 baking potato

THE ULTIMATE POTATO

Scrub the potato. Rinse the potato and pat dry. Prick holes in the potato with the tines of a fork.

Microwave on High for 6 to 8 minutes or until the potato is cooked through.

DOROTHY WIENECKE   WACO, TEXAS

FOOD FOR THOUGHT

May wrap the potato in foil and bake at 350 degrees for 45 minutes or until cooked through. Serve plain or split open and fill with butter, sour cream, chives, shredded cheese, chili, stew, soup, roast beef or any of your other favorite fillings.

SWEET POTATO CASSEROLE

YIELD: 4 TO 6 SERVINGS

Combine the sweet potatoes, sugar, eggs, vanilla, $1/2$ cup margarine and milk in a bowl and mix well. Spoon into a buttered 8-inch baking dish.

Mix the brown sugar, flour, $1/3$ cup margarine and nuts in a bowl. Sprinkle over the sweet potato mixture. Bake at 350 degrees for 30 minutes.

BETSY COLE   MONROE, MICHIGAN

2 cups mashed cooked sweet potatoes

1 cup sugar

2 eggs, beaten

1 teaspoon vanilla extract

$1/2$ cup melted margarine

$1/3$ cup milk

1 cup packed light brown sugar

$1/2$ cup flour

$1/3$ cup melted margarine

1 cup chopped nuts

VEGETABLE CASSEROLE

YIELD: 6 SERVINGS

1 (10-ounce) package frozen chopped broccoli

4 carrots, sliced

2 tablespoons margarine

2 tablespoons flour

1 cup milk

1 (5-ounce) jar Old English cheese spread

2 slices bread, crusts trimmed, cut into cubes

Cook the broccoli and carrots in a small amount of water in separate saucepans until tender-crisp. Melt the margarine in a saucepan. Add the flour, stirring constantly until blended. Add the milk, stirring until smooth. Add the cheese. Cook until the cheese is melted and the sauce is thickened and smooth, stirring constantly.

Drain the vegetables. Arrange in a 2-quart baking dish. Pour the cheese sauce over the vegetables. Arrange the bread cubes over the top. Bake at 350 degrees for 30 minutes or until the bread is toasted.

FRIEND OF HIGH/SCOPE

FOOD FOR THOUGHT

May use 1 bunch fresh broccoli instead of frozen broccoli.
Skim milk may be substituted for the whole milk.

D ESSERTS

*High/Scope conducts research in order to develop
new knowledge about education and human development.*

YIELD: 36 SERVINGS

1/2 (12-ounce) package
    vanilla wafers (36 vanilla
    wafers)
16 ounces cream cheese,
    softened
 1 cup sugar
 2 eggs
 1 tablespoon vanilla extract
 1 (21-ounce) can cherry pie
    filling, chilled
 8 ounces whipped topping
    Finely chopped nuts

INDIVIDUAL CHERRY CHEESECAKES

Place 1 vanilla wafer in each paper-lined muffin cup. Beat the cream cheese, sugar, eggs and vanilla at high speed in a mixer bowl until smooth and very creamy. Spoon 2 tablespoons of the cream cheese mixture into each prepared muffin cup.

Bake at 350 degrees for 20 to 30 minutes or until set. Let stand until cool. Spoon the cherry pie filling onto each individual cheesecake. Top each with whipped topping and sprinkle with nuts.

HIGH/SCOPE CAMP AND CONFERENCE CENTER   CLINTON, MICHIGAN

114

CHOCOLATE ÉCLAIR DESSERT

YIELD: 24 SERVINGS

Whip the pudding mix and 3 cups milk in a bowl until smooth and thick. Beat the whipping cream in a large mixer bowl until stiff. Fold in the pudding.

Line the bottom of a buttered 9x13-inch dish with crackers. Layer the pudding and remaining crackers 1/3 at a time in the prepared dish, ending with a layer of crackers. Spread the Chocolate Frosting over the top. Chill overnight.

CHOCOLATE FROSTING

2 packages liquid baking chocolate

2 tablespoons milk

2 tablespoons light corn syrup

1 teaspoon vanilla extract

1 1/2 cups confectioners' sugar

Combine the baking chocolate, 2 tablespoons milk, corn syrup and vanilla in a mixer bowl and blend well.

Add the confectioners' sugar gradually, beating constantly until smooth.

MARGARET DONAHUE   YPSILANTI, MICHIGAN

FOOD FOR THOUGHT

A great no-bake treat for summer company.

2 (4-ounce) packages vanilla instant pudding mix

3 cups milk

2 small cartons whipping cream

1 (16-ounce) package low-sodium club crackers or graham crackers
Chocolate Frosting

FROZEN CHOCOLATE MINT DESSERT

YIELD: 24 SERVINGS

1/4 cup melted butter

1 cup vanilla wafer crumbs

1/2 cup butter, softened

4 egg yolks

3 cups confectioners' sugar

3 ounces unsweetened chocolate, melted

1 1/2 teaspoons vanilla extract

2/3 cup chopped nuts

4 egg whites, stiffly beaten

1/2 gallon chocolate mint ice cream, softened

An excellent rich and refreshing summer treat.

Mix 1/4 cup butter and vanilla wafer crumbs in a bowl. Press over the bottom of a 9x13-inch dish.

Beat 1/2 cup butter, egg yolks and confectioners' sugar in a mixer bowl until smooth. Beat in the melted chocolate, vanilla and nuts. Fold in the stiffly beaten egg whites. Spread in the prepared dish. Spread the softened ice cream over the top. Freeze, covered, until firm.

EMILY KOEPP-HIGH/SCOPE DIRECTOR OF MARKETING AND FUND DEVELOPMENT
YPSILANTI, MICHIGAN

"Float and Sink" Gelatin Dessert

YIELD: 6 SERVINGS

Prepare the gelatin using the package directions. Pour into 6 clear plastic cups. Let stand for 30 minutes to cool.

Divide the fruit, marshmallows and nuts into 6 portions. Add to the gelatin in the cups and mix gently. Chill until firm.

BECKY CARSWELL   WOODBRIDGE, VIRGINIA

FOOD FOR THOUGHT

Some of the fruit in this dessert will sink and some will float. It is fun to see what happens.

2 (3-ounce) packages flavored gelatin
1/2 cup blueberries
1/2 cup sliced bananas
1/2 cup sliced strawberries
1/2 cup miniature marshmallows
1/4 cup chopped nuts

YIELD: 6 SERVINGS

1/4 cup flour

1 cup sugar

1/2 teaspoon salt

1 1/2 teaspoons grated lemon
   peel

1/4 cup lemon juice

2 egg yolks

1 cup milk

2 egg whites, stiffly beaten

LEMON PUDDING CAKE DESSERT

One of our favorite recipes, it came from Gran's World War I/Depression cookbook.

Mix the flour, sugar and salt in a mixer bowl. Add the lemon peel, lemon juice, egg yolks and milk and beat well. Fold in the stiffly beaten egg whites.

   Pour into a 1 1/2-quart baking dish or 6 custard cups. Place in a larger pan filled with enough water to reach 1 inch up the outside of the baking dish. Bake at 350 degrees for 50 minutes or until set.

CHERYL FARMER—MAYOR OF YPSILANTI   YPSILANTI, MICHIGAN

FOOD FOR THOUGHT

Serve this dessert warm in winter and cold in summer. It tastes like lemon meringue pie in a fraction of the time.

GRAPE-NUTS PUFF PUDDING

This recipe originally appeared on the Grape-Nuts cereal package in the 1940s.

Cream the butter, sugar and lemon peel in a mixer bowl. Add the egg yolks and beat until light and fluffy. Blend in the lemon juice, flour, cereal and milk. Fold in the stiffly beaten egg whites. Pour into a greased 1-quart baking dish.

Place in a larger pan partially filled with hot water. Bake at 325 degrees for 1¼ hours or until the top springs back when lightly touched.

MARGE SENNINGER–HIGH/SCOPE SENIOR EDITOR   YPSILANTI, MICHIGAN

YIELD: 4 SERVINGS

- ¼ cup butter, softened
- ½ cup sugar
- 1 teaspoon grated lemon peel
- 2 egg yolks
- 3 tablespoons lemon juice
- 2 tablespoons flour
- ¼ cup Grape-Nuts cereal
- 1 cup milk
- 2 egg whites, stiffly beaten

3 *egg whites*
1/2 *teaspoon baking powder*
1 *cup sugar*
1 *cup graham cracker crumbs*
1 *cup chopped pecans*
1 *teaspoon vanilla extract*
Fresh Berry Sauce
Whipped cream

PECAN TORTE WITH FRESH BERRY SAUCE

Beat the egg whites and baking powder in a mixer bowl until soft peaks form. Add the sugar gradually, beating until stiff peaks form. Fold in the graham cracker crumbs and pecans. Fold in the vanilla. Spread over the bottom of a greased and waxed-paper-lined 8-inch round baking pan.

Bake at 350 degrees for 25 to 30 minutes or until the top is firm and light brown. Let stand until cool. Cut into serving pieces and place on dessert plates. Spoon the Fresh Berry Sauce over the top of each serving and dollop with whipped cream.

FRESH BERRY SAUCE

1 *quart strawberries, or 1 pint raspberries*
Sugar to taste
1/2 *teaspoon cornstarch*

Rinse the strawberries and cut into slices. Combine the strawberries with water to cover in a saucepan. Add the sugar and cornstarch.

Cook until of the desired consistency, stirring constantly.

FRIEND OF HIGH/SCOPE

FOOD FOR THOUGHT

May store the unused portion of the torte, tightly covered, in the refrigerator for several days.

S N O W B A L L S

Mix the margarine and sugar in a large bowl. Add the raisins, pineapple, bananas and vanilla wafers and mix well. Stir in the nuts.

Shape into 11 balls and place each in an individual serving dish. Spread whipped cream over each ball and sprinkle with coconut. Top each with a cherry.

FRIEND OF HIGH/SCOPE

1/4 cup melted margarine

1/2 cup sugar

1/2 cup chopped raisins

1 (8-ounce) can crushed pineapple, drained

2 bananas, mashed

1 (12-ounce) package vanilla wafers, crushed

1 cup chopped nuts

Whipped cream

Shredded coconut

11 maraschino cherries

1 (2-layer) package yellow
   cake mix
1 (16-ounce) can prepared
   butterscotch pudding
2 eggs
1 cup butterscotch chips
1 cup slivered almonds

BUTTERSCOTCH PUDDING CAKE

Beat the cake mix, pudding and eggs in a mixer bowl for 2 minutes. Pour into a 9x13-inch cake pan sprayed with nonstick cooking spray. Sprinkle with butterscotch chips and almonds.

Bake at 350 degrees for 35 minutes. Cool before serving.

JAN GIFFORD—HIGH/SCOPE ELEMENTARY DIVISION SECRETARY
YPSILANTI, MICHIGAN

SURPRISE PINEAPPLE CAKE

YIELD: 15 SERVINGS

1 (1-layer) package yellow
cake mix

1/2 cup milk

8 ounces cream cheese,
softened

2 (4-ounce) packages
vanilla instant pudding
mix

2 1/2 cups milk

2 (10-ounce) cans crushed
pineapple, drained

1 envelope whipped topping
mix, prepared

1/4 cup chopped nuts

Prepare and bake cake using the package directions for a 9x13-inch cake pan. Let stand until cool. Beat 1/2 cup milk and cream cheese in a mixer bowl until smooth. Mix the pudding mix and 2 1/2 cups milk in a large bowl until smooth and thick. Add the cream cheese mixture gradually, beating constantly.

Layer the drained pineapple and pudding mixture over the cooled cake. Spread the prepared whipped topping over the top. Sprinkle with nuts. Chill in the refrigerator until serving time.

FRIEND OF HIGH/SCOPE

Chocolate Bundt Cake

Yield: 15 servings

1 (2-layer) package deep chocolate cake mix
1 (4-ounce) package chocolate instant pudding mix
1/2 cup vegetable oil
1/2 cup warm water
4 eggs
1 1/2 cups sour cream
2 cups semisweet chocolate chips

Combine the cake mix, pudding mix, vegetable oil, water, eggs and sour cream in a large mixer bowl. Beat for 2 minutes. Stir in the chocolate chips. Pour into a greased and floured bundt pan.

Bake at 350 degrees for 1 hour or until the cake tests done. Cool in the pan for several minutes. Invert onto a wire rack to cool completely. Chill, covered, in the refrigerator.

High/Scope Camp and Conference Center   Clinton, Michigan

CHOCOLATE SHEET CAKE

YIELD: 15 SERVINGS

Combine the flour and sugar in a large bowl. Bring the baking cocoa, margarine, vegetable oil and water to a boil in a saucepan, stirring occasionally. Pour the hot baking cocoa mixture over the flour mixture and mix well. Add the eggs, vanilla, salt, baking soda and buttermilk and mix well.

Pour into a greased 9x13-inch cake pan. Bake at 375 degrees for 15 minutes or until the cake tests done. Spread the warm Nutty Chocolate Frosting over the warm cake.

NUTTY CHOCOLATE FROSTING

1/2 cup margarine

3 1/2 tablespoons (heaping) baking cocoa

1/3 cup buttermilk

1/8 teaspoon salt

1 pound confectioners' sugar

1 teaspoon vanilla extract

1 cup chopped walnuts

Combine the margarine, baking cocoa, buttermilk and salt in a saucepan. Bring to a boil, stirring occasionally.

Add the confectioners' sugar and mix until smooth. Stir in the vanilla and walnuts.

HIGH/SCOPE CAMP AND CONFERENCE CENTER   CLINTON, MICHIGAN

2 cups flour

2 cups sugar

3 1/2 tablespoons (heaping) baking cocoa

1/2 cup margarine or butter

1/2 cup vegetable oil

1 cup water

2 eggs, lightly beaten

1 teaspoon vanilla extract

1/2 teaspoon salt

1 teaspoon baking soda

1/3 cup buttermilk
Nutty Chocolate Frosting

B L U E   R I B B O N   C A R R O T   C A K E

YIELD: 12 SERVINGS

2 cups flour

2 teaspoons baking soda

1/2 teaspoon salt

2 teaspoons cinnamon

3 eggs, beaten

3/4 cup vegetable oil

3/4 cup buttermilk

2 cups sugar

2 teaspoons vanilla extract

1 (8-ounce) can crushed
   pineapple, drained

2 cups grated carrots

3 1/2 ounces flaked coconut

1 cup chopped walnuts

Buttermilk Glaze
(at right)

Orange Cream Cheese
Frosting (at right)

Mix the flour, baking soda, salt and cinnamon together. Combine the eggs, vegetable oil, buttermilk, sugar and vanilla in a mixer bowl and beat until smooth. Add the flour mixture and mix well. Stir in the pineapple, carrots, coconut and chopped walnuts. Pour into 2 greased and floured 9-inch round cake pans.

Bake at 350 degrees for 35 to 40 minutes or until a wooden pick inserted near the center comes out clean. Spread the Buttermilk Glaze over the hot layers. Cool in the pans for 15 minutes. Remove to a wire rack to cool completely. Spread the Orange Cream Cheese Frosting between the layers and over the top and side of the cake. Store, covered, in the refrigerator.

BUTTERMILK GLAZE

1 cup sugar

¹/₂ teaspoon baking soda

¹/₂ cup buttermilk

¹/₂ cup butter

1 tablespoon light corn syrup

1 teaspoon vanilla extract

Combine the sugar, baking soda, buttermilk, butter and corn syrup in a saucepan. Bring to a boil. Cook for 4 minutes, stirring frequently. Remove from heat. Stir in the vanilla.

ORANGE CREAM CHEESE FROSTING

¹/₂ cup butter, softened

8 ounces cream cheese, softened

1 teaspoon vanilla extract

2 cups confectioners' sugar

1 teaspoon grated orange peel

1 teaspoon thawed orange juice concentrate

Cream the butter and cream cheese in a mixer bowl. Add the vanilla, confectioners' sugar, orange peel and orange juice concentrate. Beat until very light and fluffy and of the desired consistency.

HIGH/SCOPE CAMP AND CONFERENCE CENTER   CLINTON, MICHIGAN

B O N B O N S

YIELD: 2 TO 2½ DOZEN

4 cups crisp rice cereal

½ cup margarine, softened

2 cups creamy peanut butter

1 pound confectioners' sugar

1 (8-ounce) bar milk chocolate

1 cup semisweet chocolate chips

½ (6-ounce) cake paraffin

Crush the cereal lightly in a plastic food storage bag. Beat the margarine, peanut butter and confectioners' sugar in a bowl. Add the crushed cereal and mix well. Shape into ¾-inch balls. Place on a tray. Chill for 1 hour.

Melt the chocolate bar, chocolate chips and paraffin over hot water in a double boiler and mix well. Dip the peanut butter balls into the chocolate mixture to coat. Place on a waxed-paper-lined surface. Let stand until cool.

FRIEND OF HIGH/SCOPE

FOOD FOR THOUGHT

These bonbons may be frozen.

PRALINES À LA ORLEANS

YIELD: 30 TO 60 SERVINGS

Pralines, the traditional New Orleans candy, are even easier to make using the microwave.

Mix the whipping cream and brown sugar in a 4-quart microwave-safe bowl. Microwave on High for 13 minutes or until the mixture reaches 234 to 240 degrees on a candy thermometer, soft-ball stage, stirring 2 times.

Stir in the margarine, vanilla and pecans. Beat for 1 minute. Drop by teaspoonfuls onto a foil-lined padded surface. Let stand until cool.

JANIS DERING   CHALMETTE, LOUISIANA

1 cup whipping cream

1 pound light brown sugar

2 tablespoons margarine, softened

1/4 teaspoon vanilla extract

2 cups pecan halves

CARAMEL BROWNIES

YIELD: 40 SERVINGS

40 caramels

$1/2$ cup evaporated milk

1 (2-layer) package German chocolate cake mix

$3/4$ cup butter, softened

$1/3$ cup evaporated milk

2 cups milk chocolate chips

Melt the caramels with $1/2$ cup evaporated milk in a saucepan, stirring constantly. Mix the cake mix, butter and $1/3$ cup evaporated milk in a bowl and mix well. Press half the mixture over the bottom of a greased 9x13-inch baking pan.

Bake at 350 degrees for 10 minutes. Sprinkle with the chocolate chips. Pour the melted caramel mixture over the chocolate chips. Crumble the remaining cake mix mixture over the top. Bake for 20 minutes. Let stand until cool. Cut into bars.

BECKY CARSWELL   WOODBRIDGE, VIRGINIA

FUDGE BROWNIES

YIELD: 9 TO 12 SERVINGS

Place the butter and unsweetened chocolate in a microwave-safe dish. Microwave on High until melted. Add the sugar and stir until dissolved. Beat in the eggs 1 at a time. Stir in the vanilla. Add the flour and nuts and mix well. Spoon into a nonstick 8x8-inch baking pan.

Bake at 350 degrees for 25 minutes or until a wooden pick inserted near the center comes out clean. Let stand until cool. Cut into bars.

NANCY L. HEYWOOD—HIGH/SCOPE HUMAN RESOURCES REPRESENTATIVE
YPSILANTI, MICHIGAN

FOOD FOR THOUGHT

May substitute 6 tablespoons baking cocoa and 2 tablespoons vegetable oil for the unsweetened chocolate.

1/2 cup butter or margarine

2 ounces unsweetened chocolate

1 cup sugar

2 eggs

1 teaspoon vanilla extract

1/2 cup flour

1/2 cup chopped nuts (optional)

YIELD: 48 SERVINGS

CHOCOLATE CHESS BARS

1 (2-layer) package devil's
  food cake mix

1 egg

1/2 cup melted light
  margarine

1 tablespoon water

8 ounces cream cheese,
  softened

1 pound confectioners' sugar

3 egg whites

1 teaspoon vanilla extract

Combine the cake mix, 1 egg, margarine and water in a bowl and mix well. Press over the bottom of a 9x13-inch baking pan sprayed with nonstick cooking spray.

Beat the cream cheese, confectioners' sugar and egg whites in a mixer bowl until smooth and creamy. Beat in the vanilla. Pour into the prepared pan. Bake at 350 degrees for 45 minutes or until the top is golden brown. Cool and cut into bars.

FRIEND OF HIGH/SCOPE

CHOCOLATE CHIP COOKIES

YIELD: 5 DOZEN

This recipe is based on a traditional drop cookie recipe that I have adapted to include lots of chocolate. I like it because the cookies don't come out greasy. These cookies freeze well—if you have any left.

Sift the flour, baking powder, baking cocoa and cinnamon together. Cream the butter, sugar, brown sugar and vanilla in a mixer bowl until light and fluffy. Add the eggs 1 at a time, beating constantly. Add the sifted dry ingredients alternately with the milk, beating well after each addition. Stir in the chocolate chips.

Drop by tablespoonfuls onto a lightly greased cookie sheet. Bake at 325 degrees for 15 minutes or until the cookies test done. Remove to a wire rack to cool.

ANNE HUDON—HIGH/SCOPE CONFERENCE COORDINATOR AND ASSISTANT TO THE REGISTRAR
YPSILANTI, MICHIGAN

4 cups flour

5 teaspoons baking powder

3 tablespoons (heaping) baking cocoa

1 teaspoon cinnamon

3/4 cup unsalted butter, softened

1/2 cup sugar

1 cup packed light brown sugar

1 tablespoon vanilla extract

2 eggs, beaten

3/4 cup milk

3 cups semisweet or dark chocolate chips

COOKIE PIZZA

Children love this recipe.

Cream the margarine, brown sugar and sugar in a mixer bowl. Beat in the egg and vanilla until light and fluffy. Add the flour, baking soda and salt and beat until smooth. Stir in the chocolate chips. Press over the bottom of a pizza pan. Sprinkle the miniature candies and walnuts over the top.

Bake at 350 degrees for 15 to 20 minutes or until golden brown. Remove to a wire rack to cool.

JEAN LUGINBUHL   ROANOKE, ILLINOIS

1/2 cup margarine, softened

3/4 cup packed brown sugar

3 tablespoons sugar

1 egg

1 1/2 teaspoons vanilla extract

1 1/2 cups flour

3/4 teaspoons baking soda

1/2 teaspoon salt

3/4 cup chocolate chips

1/4 cup miniature M & M's Chocolate Candies

1/4 cup chopped walnuts (optional)

LEMON BARS

Combine the margarine, confectioners' sugar and 1 cup flour in a bowl and mix well. Press over the bottom of a 9x9-inch baking pan. Bake at 350 degrees for 15 minutes.

Beat the sugar and eggs in a mixer bowl. Add the lemon juice and lemon peel and mix well. Pour over the baked layer. Sprinkle with a mixture of 2 tablespoons flour and baking powder. Bake for 25 minutes or until set. Let stand to cool completely before cutting into bars.

FRIEND OF HIGH/SCOPE

1/2 cup margarine, softened
1/2 cup confectioners' sugar
1 cup flour
1 cup sugar
2 eggs, beaten
2 tablespoons lemon juice
1 tablespoon lemon peel
2 tablespoons flour
1/2 teaspoon baking powder

137

DOUBLE CHOCOLATE OATMEAL COOKIES

1 1/2 cups sugar

1 cup margarine, softened

1 egg

1/4 cup water

1 teaspoon vanilla extract

1 1/4 cups flour

1/3 cup baking cocoa

1/2 teaspoon baking soda

1/2 teaspoon salt

3 cups quick-cooking oats

8 ounces chocolate chips

1/2 cup crisp rice cereal

Beat the sugar, margarine, egg, water and vanilla in a mixer bowl until smooth. Add the flour, baking cocoa, baking soda and salt and mix well. Stir in the oats, chocolate chips and cereal just until mixed. Add a small amount of milk or additional flour if needed for the desired consistency. Drop by spoonfuls 2 inches apart onto an ungreased cookie sheet.

Bake at 350 degrees for 10 to 12 minutes or until firm. Do not overbake. Remove to a wire rack to cool.

HIGH/SCOPE CAMP AND CONFERENCE CENTER   CLINTON, MICHIGAN

OATMEAL AND RAISIN COOKIES

A more healthful improvement to an old family favorite recipe.

Bring the raisins and water to a boil in a saucepan. Cook until the raisins are plumped. Remove from heat and let stand until cool.

Combine the brown sugar, sugar, canola oil, egg substitute and vanilla in a bowl and mix well. Add the whole wheat flour, all-purpose flour, baking powder, baking soda, salt, cinnamon and nutmeg and mix well. Stir in the oats, plumped raisins and walnuts. Let stand for 15 minutes. Drop by spoonfuls 2 inches apart onto a nonstick cookie sheet.

Bake at 350 degrees for 12 to 15 minutes or until golden brown. Remove to a wire rack to cool.

ARTHUR WALLGREN   ROSLYN, WASHINGTON

YIELD: 72 SERVINGS

1 cup raisins

2 tablespoons water

1 cup packed brown sugar

1 cup sugar

3/4 cup canola oil

1/2 cup egg substitute, or 4 egg whites

1 teaspoon vanilla extract

1 cup whole wheat flour

1 cup all-purpose flour

1 teaspoon baking powder

1 teaspoon baking soda

1/2 teaspoon salt

1 teaspoon cinnamon

1/2 teaspoon nutmeg

2 cups rolled oats

1 cup chopped walnuts

PUDDING S'MORES

YIELD: 12 SERVINGS

1/2 cup peanut butter

1 1/2 cups milk

1 (4-ounce) package vanilla instant pudding mix

24 graham crackers

Quick and so good.

Place the peanut butter in a mixer bowl. Add the milk gradually, beating constantly until smooth. Beat in the pudding mix until smooth. Let stand for 5 minutes or until thick.

Spread the filling over half the graham crackers. Top with the remaining graham crackers. Freeze, individually wrapped in plastic wrap, until firm.

BECKY CARSWELL   WOODBRIDGE, VIRGINIA

INTERNATIONAL COOKING

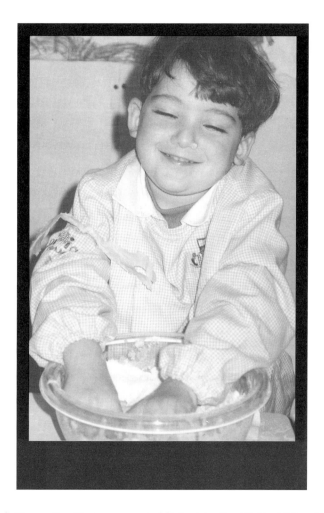

*High/Scope Institutes are established in the United Kingdom,
the Netherlands, Singapore, and Mexico.*

YIELD: 16 TO 32 SERVINGS

8 to 16 ounces mozzarella
cheese
Extra-virgin olive oil
Crushed or minced garlic
to taste
Red pepper flakes or
cayenne to taste
Oregano to taste

BOCCONCINI

Quick, easy and inexpensive. This hors d'oeuvre may be prepared well in advance of serving.

Shape the cheese into balls using a melon ball scoop or a metal measuring teaspoon. Combine the olive oil, garlic, red pepper flakes and oregano in a jar with a tightfitting lid. Cover with the lid and shake to mix well. Pour over the cheese balls in a bowl, turning to coat.

Marinate, covered, in the refrigerator for several hours or up to 3 days, stirring frequently. Drain and spoon into a serving bowl. Serve with wooden picks.

WINIFRED S. NEILL   PORTLAND, OREGON

FOOD FOR THOUGHT

The flavor is enhanced the longer the marinating time. Vary the herbs according to taste.

BLACK BEAN AND ARTICHOKE CHILI

YIELD: 4 SERVINGS

Sauté the onions, carrot, yellow pepper and garlic in the orange juice in a stockpot. Stir in the cumin, cilantro and chili powder. Cook over medium heat for 4 minutes, stirring frequently. Stir in a mixture of the water and bouillon granules. Add the beans, chiles, artichokes, undrained tomatoes and maple syrup and mix well. Cook over low heat for 30 minutes, stirring occasionally. Ladle over brown rice in chili bowls.

Garnish each serving with additional chopped fresh cilantro and nonfat sour cream or shredded soy Monterey Jack cheese.

ANN J. ROCHFORD   COLUMBIA, MARYLAND

$1^1/2$ cups chopped onions

$1/2$ cup chopped carrot

$1/2$ cup chopped yellow or green bell pepper

2 large cloves of garlic, chopped

$1/2$ cup orange juice

2 teaspoons cumin

1 teaspoon chopped fresh cilantro

$1/4$ teaspoon chili powder

2 cups water

2 teaspoons vegetable bouillon granules

2 (16-ounce) cans black beans, rinsed, drained

$1/2$ cup chopped mild green chiles

1 (15-ounce) can artichoke hearts, rinsed, drained, cut into quarters

1 (15-ounce) can crushed tomatoes

2 teaspoons maple syrup

Hot cooked brown rice

GROUNDNUT STEW

YIELD: 6 SERVINGS

1½ to 2 pounds chicken parts

3 medium onions, finely chopped

3 to 6 hot peppers, crushed

1 (12-ounce) can tomato paste

½ cup peanut oil

9 to 12 ounces smooth natural peanut butter

2½ to 3½ cups water

2 teaspoons salt

2 bouillon cubes

3 to 6 tablespoons flour

1 to 2 cups water

Juice of 1 small lime or lemon

½ head cabbage, coarsely shredded (optional)

2 to 3 zucchini, chopped (optional)

1 eggplant, chopped (optional)

Groundnut Stew, known as Tio Durango in Mandinka, is one of the staples of West Africa. It is not uncommon for this delectable commodity to be served four times a week for lunch and dinner. Traditionally, this dish, like most, is served from a large bowl with the participants gathered around. Everybody eats with their right hand. Beginners beware, the Groundnut Stew is very hot and can burn your fingers if eaten with your hands.

Rinse the chicken and pat dry. Combine the onions, hot peppers and tomato paste in a bowl and mix well. Heat the peanut oil in a large saucepan until hot. Add the onion mixture. Cook for 5 minutes, stirring constantly. Combine the peanut butter and ½ cup of the water in a bowl and mix well. Stir into the onion mixture. Mix in 1 cup of the water. Cook over medium heat for 15 minutes, stirring occasionally and adding the remaining 1 to 2 cups water. Add the salt and bouillon cubes and mix well. Cook for 10 minutes, stirring occasionally.

Add just enough flour until of the desired consistency, stirring constantly. Add 1 to 2 cups water and mix well. Cook for 10 minutes, stirring occasionally. Stir in the lime juice. Add the chicken and mix well. Add additional water to cover the chicken. Cook, covered, over medium-high heat for 20 minutes, stirring frequently.

Add the cabbage, zucchini and eggplant and mix well. Add additional water as needed to cover the vegetables and chicken. Cook over medium-high heat for 20 minutes or until the chicken is cooked through, stirring occasionally. Ladle over rice, couscous or fufu in a large serving bowl.

JOHN KENNETH WEISS (A.K.A. KEBBA TOURAY)—HIGH/SCOPE DIRECTOR, ADOLESCENT DIVISION   YPSILANTI, MICHIGAN

FOOD FOR THOUGHT

May substitute 2 to 4 teaspoons crushed dried red peppers for the fresh hot peppers and cubed beef for the chicken.

SENEGALAISE

Rinse the chicken and pat dry. Sauté the onion, celery and apple in the butter in a saucepan until tender. Stir in the flour and curry powder with a wooden spoon. Cook over low heat for 5 minutes, stirring frequently. Add the chicken, broth, cloves and cinnamon stick. Simmer, covered, for 30 minutes.

Remove the chicken breast to a bowl with a slotted spoon and chop. Discard the cloves and cinnamon stick. Process the onion mixture in a blender. Return to the saucepan. Stir in the chicken. Add the whipping cream gradually, stirring constantly. Cook just until heated through, stirring constantly; do not boil. Ladle into soup bowls. Sprinkle each serving with coconut.

SKIP SACKETT   FONTANA, WISCONSIN

FOOD FOR THOUGHT

To toast coconut, spread shredded coconut on a baking sheet. Toast at 300 degrees for 20 minutes or until golden brown.

YIELD: 4 SERVINGS

1 boneless skinless chicken breast
1 cup chopped onion
2 ribs celery, chopped
1 medium apple, peeled, chopped
1/4 cup butter
3 tablespoons flour
1 tablespoon curry powder
3 1/2 cups chicken broth
3 whole cloves
1 cinnamon stick
1 cup whipping cream
Toasted coconut

YIELD: 6 TO 8 SERVINGS

1 pound ground beef

1 can hot dog chili without
beans

2 (10-ounce) cans enchilada
sauce

Vegetable oil

1 package tortillas

Shredded Cheddar cheese

1 medium onion, grated

1/4 cup water

Shredded Monterey Jack
cheese

Finely chopped black
olives

E N C H I L A D A S

Brown the ground beef in a skillet, stirring until crumbly; drain. Stir in the chili. Pour 1 of the cans of the enchilada sauce into a bowl.

Heat the oil in a skillet until hot. Fry the tortillas in the hot oil for 30 seconds per side or until brown. Dip the tortillas 1 at a time into the enchilada sauce. Spoon 1½ tablespoons of the ground beef mixture onto each tortilla. Sprinkle with some of the Cheddar cheese and the onion. Roll to enclose the filling. Arrange seam side down in a 9x13-inch baking dish.

Combine the remaining can of enchilada sauce and the water in a bowl and mix well. Pour over the enchiladas. Sprinkle with the remaining Cheddar cheese, Monterey Jack Cheese and olives. Bake, covered, at 350 degrees for 30 minutes or until bubbly.

EMILY KOEPP-HIGH/SCOPE DIRECTOR OF MARKETING AND FUND DEVELOPMENT
YPSILANTI, MICHIGAN

BENACHIN

Benachin or Jollof Rice is a common dish in West Africa. It is often served at naming ceremonies, weddings, and other happy occasions. Traditionally this dish, like most, is served from a large bowl with the participants gathered around. Everybody eats with their right hand.

Rinse the chicken and pat dry. Sprinkle with the salt and black pepper. Heat the peanut oil in a 3-quart saucepan until hot. Fry the chicken in the hot oil for 10 to 15 minutes or until almost cooked through. Remove the chicken to a bowl with a slotted spoon, reserving the pan drippings. Cool the pan drippings slightly.

Stir the onions and tomato paste into the pan drippings. Add the garlic, hot peppers, salt and black pepper. Mix in the water. Cook over medium-high heat until brown, stirring constantly. Add the chicken, cabbage, zucchini and eggplant and mix well. Add additional water to cover the chicken and vegetables. Boil for 35 to 40 minutes, stirring frequently. Remove the chicken and vegetables to a bowl with a slotted spoon, reserving the pan drippings.

Add the rice to the reserved pan drippings. Cook until tender, stirring occasionally. Stir in the chicken and vegetables. Spoon into a large serving bowl.

JOHN KENNETH WEISS (A.K.A. KEBBA TOURAY)—HIGH/SCOPE DIRECTOR,
ADOLESCENT DIVISION   YPSILANTI, MICHIGAN

FOOD FOR THOUGHT

May substitute cubed beef for the chicken and 2 to 4 teaspoons crushed dried red peppers for the fresh hot peppers.

1½ to 2 pounds chicken parts

2 teaspoons salt

1½ to 2 teaspoons black pepper

1 cup peanut oil

3 medium onions, chopped

1 (12-ounce) can tomato paste

2 to 4 cloves of garlic, crushed

3 to 6 hot peppers, crushed
Salt and black pepper to taste

2 cups water

½ head cabbage, shredded (optional)

2 to 3 zucchini, sliced (optional)

1 eggplant, coarsely chopped (optional)

2½ to 3 cups rice

YIELD: 8 SERVINGS

CHINESE CHICKEN WITH CASHEWS

2 pounds boneless skinless chicken breasts

1/3 cup sesame oil

1/3 cup rice vinegar

1/4 cup dry sherry

2 cloves of garlic, finely chopped

8 ounces snow peas, trimmed

1/3 cup soy sauce

1 1/2 teaspoons cornstarch

1/3 cup hoisin sauce

1 tablespoon sugar (optional)

2 tablespoons grated fresh gingerroot

2 tablespoons peanut oil

1 (7-ounce) can water chestnuts, drained, sliced

8 ounces mushrooms, sliced

1 1/2 cups chopped cashews

3/4 to 1 cup sliced scallions with tops

3 cups rice, cooked

Rinse the chicken and pat dry. Cut into 1-inch pieces. Combine the sesame oil, rice vinegar, sherry and garlic in a bowl and mix well. Add the chicken. Marinate, covered, in the refrigerator for 1 hour. Drain, reserving the marinade.

Blanch the snow peas in boiling water in a saucepan for 30 seconds and drain. Combine the soy sauce and cornstarch in a bowl and mix well. Stir in the hoisin sauce, sugar and ginger. Heat the peanut oil in a wok or heavy saucepan over high heat. Add the chicken.

Stir-fry for 3 to 4 minutes or until the chicken is cooked through. Stir in the reserved marinade and soy sauce mixture. Add the snow peas, water chestnuts, mushrooms and cashews and mix well. Cook for 5 to 6 minutes or until the mixture is heated through, stirring frequently. Add the scallions and mix well. Stir-fry for 1 minute. Serve over the hot cooked rice.

FRIEND OF HIGH/SCOPE

CATALAN CHICK-PEAS

YIELD: 6 SERVINGS

This dish is popular in homes in Barcelona and Catalonia. This dish normally requires a fresh sausage which is a specialty of Catalonia, but I have suggested some substitutions. If you have a sausage making machine you can make them easily (see below).

Sort and rinse the chick-peas. Combine the chick-peas with enough water to cover in a bowl. Soak overnight. Drain and rinse. Combine the chick-peas and baking soda with enough water to cover in a saucepan. Bring to a boil; reduce heat. Simmer, covered, for 1 hour.

Simmer the sausage in water to cover in a saucepan for 20 minutes or prick the casings of the sausage with a fork and fry in a skillet. Cut the sausage into 1- to 2-inch slices. Simmer the bacon in water in a saucepan for 10 minutes. Drain and rinse.

Brown the bacon, onion, garlic and green pepper in the olive oil in a skillet. Stir in the tomatoes, nutmeg, salt and pepper. Cook, covered, for 10 minutes, stirring occasionally. Stir in the sausage. Drain the chick-peas, reserving 2 cups of the liquid. Combine the chick-peas, reserved liquid and the tomato mixture in a bowl and mix well. Season with salt and pepper. Spoon into a baking pan. Bake, covered, at 375 degrees Fahrenheit or 190 degrees Celsius for 1¹/₂ hours, stirring occasionally. Ladle into soup bowls.

DOLORS IDUARTE-CONSELL SUPERIOR D'AVALUACIÓ   BARCELONA, SPAIN

FOOD FOR THOUGHT

To make the sausage, combine 250 grams (8 ounces) pork with 50 to 75 grams (1¹/₂ to 2¹/₂ ounces) pork fat in a bowl and mix well. Stir in a few tablespoons of white wine. Season with salt, pepper, cinnamon or nutmeg, ground cloves and crushed thyme. Stuff the sausage into casings. Hang the sausage in an airy environment for 24 hours. Cook in boiling water in a stockpot. Serve hot or cold.

Ingredients:

300 grams (10 ounces) dried chick-peas

¹/₄ teaspoon baking soda

250 grams (8 ounces) Catalonian sausage or fresh pork sausage

150 grams (5 ounces) slab bacon or lean salt pork

1 tablespoon olive oil, lard or sausage drippings

1 large onion, chopped

1 teaspoon finely chopped garlic

1 large green bell pepper, finely chopped

4 large tomatoes, peeled, seeded, chopped

Freshly grated nutmeg or cinnamon

Salt and pepper to taste

MANDARIN PORK STIR-FRY

YIELD: 6 SERVINGS

2 tablespoons cornstarch

1 1/4 cups water

1/3 cup soy sauce

1/3 cup corn syrup

1/3 to 1/2 teaspoon crushed
dried red pepper

1 pound pork tenderloin

2 cloves of garlic, minced

4 tablespoons peanut oil

2 cups chopped broccoli

2 onions, thinly sliced

2 carrots, cut into 2-inch
strips

1 (7-ounce) can water
chestnuts, cut into halves
or quarters

8 ounces mushrooms

1 cup rice, cooked

Blend the cornstarch and water in a bowl. Stir in the soy sauce, corn syrup and red pepper. Cut the pork into thin strips. Stir-fry the pork with the garlic in 2 tablespoons of the oil in a wok or large skillet for 5 minutes or until cooked through. Remove from the wok.

Heat the remaining 2 tablespoons oil in the wok. Add the broccoli, onions and carrots. Stir-fry for 3 minutes. Add the water chestnuts and mushrooms. Stir-fry for 1 minute or until the vegetables are tender-crisp. Return the pork to the wok. Stir in the cornstarch mixture. Cook for 12 minutes or until thickened to the desired consistency, stirring constantly. Serve over the rice.

FRIEND OF HIGH/SCOPE

Moussaka

YIELD: 8 SERVINGS

Cut the eggplant into slices lengthwise. Brown the eggplant slices on both sides in the shortening in a skillet and remove to a platter. Add 2 tablespoons butter, onions and garlic to the skillet. Sauté just until wilted. Stir in the ground lamb, thyme, oregano, tomatoes and 1 teaspoon salt. Simmer, covered, for 30 minutes. Let stand until cool. Stir in the unbeaten egg whites and half the bread crumbs. Sprinkle the remaining bread crumbs into a greased baking dish. Layer the eggplant and lamb mixture 1/2 at a time in the prepared dish.

Blend the flour and 2 tablespoons melted butter in a saucepan. Stir in the milk and 1/2 teaspoon salt. Cook over low heat until smooth and thickened, stirring constantly. Stir a small amount of the hot mixture into the egg yolks; stir the egg yolks into the hot mixture. Season with the nutmeg. Pour over the layers in the baking dish. Sprinkle with the Parmesan cheese. Bake at 350 degrees for 1 hour.

FRIEND OF HIGH/SCOPE

2 eggplant
1/2 cup shortening
2 tablespoons butter
4 medium onions, chopped
3 cloves of garlic, chopped
1 pound ground lamb
1/2 teaspoon thyme
1/2 teaspoon oregano
1/2 cup canned tomatoes
1 teaspoon salt
2 egg whites
1/2 cup bread crumbs
2 tablespoons flour
2 tablespoons melted butter
1 1/2 cups milk
1/2 teaspoon salt
2 egg yolks
1/4 teaspoon nutmeg
4 teaspoons grated
  Parmesan cheese

S P I C Y   L A M B

YIELD: 4 SERVINGS

400 grams, or 1(14-ounce) can peeled tomatoes

2 pounds boneless lamb

3 tablespoons yogurt

1 teaspoon garlic paste or chopped garlic

1 teaspoon ginger paste or chopped gingerroot

1 green chile, chopped, or 1/2 teaspoon chile paste

1/2 teaspoon salt

1 pound onions, chopped

5 tablespoons vegetable oil

2 teaspoons coriander or cumin powder

1/2 teaspoon red hot chili powder

1/2 teaspoon turmeric

1 tablespoon chopped fresh coriander leaves

1/3 teaspoon ground cloves

1/3 teaspoon cardamom

1/3 teaspoon cinnamon

Drain the tomatoes, reserving the juice. Chop the tomatoes. Combine the reserved tomato juice, lamb, yogurt, garlic paste, ginger paste, chile and salt in a saucepan and mix well. Cook for 40 to 45 minutes or until the lamb is tender, stirring occasionally.

Sauté the onions in the oil in a saucepan until light brown. Stir in the tomatoes, coriander powder, chili powder and turmeric. Cook over low heat for 5 minutes, stirring frequently. Add the lamb mixture and mix well. Cook over low heat for 5 to 10 minutes, stirring occasionally. Stir in the fresh coriander, cloves, cardamom and cinnamon. Let stand for 5 minutes to allow the flavors to marry. Serve with hot cooked rice and/or French bread.

AMIR BHATIA–HIGH/SCOPE BOARD OF DIRECTORS   LONDON, ENGLAND

Catalan Spinach

YIELD: 4 SERVINGS

*The first Catalan written references to spinach date from the twelfth century.
It is referred to as an austere and Lent dish before the nineteenth century, when it was first
conceived as a dish to be prepared in different exquisite ways.*

Cook the spinach in boiling salted water in a saucepan for 8 minutes. Drain and chop. Sauté the garlic in the olive oil in a skillet until brown; push to side of skillet. Add the pine nuts and mix well. Sauté for 1 minute. Stir in the currants. Arrange the undrained pine nuts and currants in a decorative pattern over the bottom of a mold.

Sauté the spinach in the pan drippings in the skillet over low heat for 5 minutes. Spoon into the prepared mold and press lightly. Let stand for several minutes. Invert onto a serving platter. Serve with fried toast.

Dolors Iduarte-Consell Superior D'Avaluació   Barcelona, Spain

1½ kilograms (3 pounds) spinach

Salt to taste

1 clove of garlic

5 soupspoons olive oil

100 grams (3½ ounces) pine nuts

100 grams (3½ ounces) currants

YIELD: 8 SERVINGS

6 tablespoons butter

2 eggs, beaten

2²/₃ cups cooked rice

²/₃ cup chopped green onions

²/₃ cup chopped red bell
pepper

²/₃ cup water

¹/₄ cup soy sauce

FRIED RICE

Heat the butter in a skillet until melted. Stir in the eggs. Cook until almost set. Stir in the rice, green onions and red pepper.

Cook for 5 minutes, stirring frequently. Add the water and soy sauce and mix well. Cook for 2 minutes, stirring frequently.

HIGH/SCOPE CAMP AND CONFERENCE CENTER   CLINTON, MICHIGAN

Salsa Romesco

YIELD: 10 OUNCES

A strong rich spicy sauce that reminds me of the Mexican sauce "cascabel."
Serve on grilled and poached fish, grilled meat and hot or cold shellfish.

Combine the hot pepper with enough water to cover in a bowl. Let stand until soft; drain. Discard the seeds.

Blanch the almonds in boiling water. Drain and discard the skins. Arrange the almonds in a single layer on a baking sheet. Toast in a moderate oven until golden brown. Process in a blender until finely ground.

Combine the hot pepper, garlic, paprika, tomatoes and salt in a blender container. Process until smooth. Add the olive oil gradually, processing constantly until of the consistency of light cream. Add the desired amount of vinegar. Process until blended. Pour into a serving bowl. Fold in the almonds.

Dolors Iduarte-Consell Superior D'Avaluació   Barcelona, Spain

1 dried hot pepper

75 grams (2 ounces) whole shelled almonds

1 teaspoon finely chopped garlic

1 teaspoon paprika

2 or 3 tomatoes, grilled, peeled, seeded, mashed

Salt to taste

120 milliliters (4 ounces) olive oil

2 to 3 tablespoons wine vinegar

ARROZ CON DULCE

YIELD: 8 TO 12 SERVINGS

2 cups medium-grain rice

2 coconuts

2 cups water

Chopped gingerroot to taste

4 to 6 cinnamon sticks

2 cups sugar

1 cup raisins

1/4 cup butter

1 teaspoon salt

Ground cinnamon to taste

This dish is traditionally made in Puerto Rico during the Christmas holidays.

Soak the rice in enough water to cover in a bowl for 1 hour; drain. Grate the coconut pulp and place in a colander. Press to extract the liquid. Combine the coconut liquid with enough water to equal 6 cups. Discard the coconut pulp.

Combine 2 cups water, gingerroot and cinnamon sticks in a saucepan. Boil for 30 minutes. Stir in the coconut liquid. Stir in the sugar, raisins, butter, salt and rice. Cook over medium heat for 40 minutes or until the rice is tender, stirring occasionally with a wooden spoon. Spoon into a serving bowl and sprinkle with ground cinnamon.

MARÍA GARCÍA   BRONX, NEW YORK

BAKLAVA

YIELD: 45 SERVINGS

Combine 2 cups sugar, honey, water and lemon juice in a saucepan. Bring to a boil; reduce heat. Cook until of a syrup consistency, stirring frequently. Let stand until cool. Combine the walnuts, $1/2$ cup sugar, cinnamon and cloves in a bowl and mix well.

Brush the bottom of a 12x17-inch baking pan with some of the butter. Layer 8 sheets of the phyllo pastry in the prepared pan, brushing each sheet with butter. Spread with $1/2$ of the walnut mixture. Layer with 8 more sheets of the pastry, brushing each sheet with melted butter. Spread with the remaining walnut mixture. Top with the remaining phyllo sheets, brushing each sheet with melted butter. Cut into diamonds with a sharp knife.

Bake at 325 degrees for 25 to 30 minutes or until golden brown. Drizzle with the syrup. Let stand until cool. Place the baklava in individual foil cups or arrange on a serving platter.

HIGH/SCOPE CAMP AND CONFERENCE CENTER   CLINTON, MICHIGAN

2 cups sugar

1 cup honey

$1/2$ cup water

1 tablespoon lemon juice

1 pound walnuts or almonds, blanched, finely chopped

$1/2$ cup sugar

$1/2$ teaspoon cinnamon

$1/8$ teaspoon ground cloves

2 cups melted unsalted butter

1 (1-pound) package phyllo pastry

ALMOND APRICOT BISCOTTI

2³/₄ cups sifted flour

1¹/₂ cups sugar

¹/₂ cup unsalted butter, cut
   into pieces, chilled

2¹/₂ teaspoons baking powder

1 teaspoon salt

1 teaspoon ground ginger

3¹/₂ ounces imported white
   chocolate, broken

1²/₃ cups whole almonds,
   toasted

2 large eggs

5 tablespoons apricot
   brandy

2 teaspoons almond extract

1 (6-ounce) package dried
   apricots, chopped

Line a cookie sheet with foil. Brush with butter and coat with flour. Combine 2³/₄ cups flour, sugar, butter, baking powder, salt and ginger in a food processor container. Process until a fine meal forms. Add the white chocolate. Process until finely chopped. Add the almonds. Pulse 6 to 8 times or until coarsely chopped.

Beat the eggs, brandy and flavoring in a bowl until blended. Add the flour mixture and apricots, stirring until a moist dough forms. Drop dough by spoonfuls into three 12-inch-long strips on the prepared cookie sheet. Shape each dough strip into a 2-inch-wide log using moistened fingertips. Chill for 30 minutes or until firm.

Place the cookie sheet on the center oven rack. Bake at 350 degrees for 30 minutes or until golden brown. Cool on the cookie sheet on a wire rack. Transfer logs to a work surface. Cut each log crosswise into ³/₄-inch slices. Arrange ¹/₂ of the cookies cut side down on a cookie sheet. Bake at 300 degrees for 10 minutes. Turn over the cookies. Bake for 10 minutes longer. Remove to a wire rack to cool. Repeat the process with the remaining cookies.

BONNIE NEUGEBAUER   REDMOND, WASHINGTON

P F E F F E R N Ü E S S E

Sift the flour, baking soda, cinnamon, cloves and ginger together. Cream the margarine and sugar in a mixer bowl until light and fluffy. Beat in the egg, corn syrup and oil of anise. Add half the flour mixture and mix well. Knead in the remaining flour mixture on a lightly floured surface. Chill in an airtight container in the refrigerator overnight.

Roll the dough into thin ropes on a lightly floured surface. Cut the ropes into $1/2$-inch-thick slices using a sharp knife. Place on a cookie sheet. Bake at 350 degrees for 7 minutes. Remove to a wire rack to cool.

FRIEND OF HIGH/SCOPE

FOOD FOR THOUGHT

These "peppernuts" can be made as small as peanuts, aged in cheesecloth sacks for several weeks to dry and crisp, and served for crunchy snacks.

$3^1/2$ *cups flour*
2 *teaspoons baking soda*
1 *teaspoon ground cinnamon*
1 *teaspoon ground cloves*
1 *teaspoon ground ginger*
1 *cup margarine, softened*
$1^1/2$ *cups sugar*
1 *egg, beaten*
2 *tablespoons light corn syrup*
$1/2$ *teaspoon oil of anise*

YIELD: 6 TO 8 SERVINGS

8 *egg yolks*
250 *grams (8 ounces) sugar*
50 *grams (1³/₄ ounces) flour*
Vanilla extract to taste
1 *liter (1 quart) milk*
50 *grams (1³/₄ ounces) sugar*

CREMA CATALANA

Combine the egg yolks, 250 grams sugar, flour and vanilla in a saucepan and mix well. Add the milk gradually, stirring constantly. Cook until thickened, stirring constantly; do not boil. Pour on a platter. Let stand until cool.

Sprinkle with 50 grams sugar. Burn with a red-hot iron until the sugar caramelizes.

DOLORS IDUARTE-CONSELL SUPERIOR D'AVALUACIÓ   BARCELONA, SPAIN

PIZZELLE

YIELD: 36 SERVINGS

Beat the sugar and eggs in a bowl until blended. Add the butter and mix well. Stir in the vanilla. Add a mixture of the flour and baking powder and mix well.

Pour about 1/4 cup of the batter at a time onto a hot pizzelle iron. Bake using manufacturer's instructions.

KELLY HAMILTON   PITTSBURGH, PENNSYLVANIA

2 cups sugar

6 eggs

1 cup melted butter

Vanilla extract or whiskey to taste

7 cups flour

4 teaspoons baking powder

YIELD: 12 TO 15 SERVINGS

60 dag (21 ounces) fine-grain
 dry wheat flour, heated

6 dag (2 ounces) cake yeast

2 tablespoons lukewarm
 milk

1 teaspoon sugar

10 dag (3.5 ounces) butter,
 softened

3 egg yolks

10 dag (3.5 ounces) sugar

2.5 to 3 deciliters (1.05 cups
 to 1.27 cups) milk, heated

2 tablespoons dark rum

Grated peel of 1 lemon

1/8 teaspoon salt

POTICA

Pronounced as paw-tee-tzah, with a stress on tee.

Sift the flour into a bowl. Cover and set in a warm place if the flour has not been heated. Crumble the yeast into a bowl. Add 2 tablespoons lukewarm milk and 1 teaspoon sugar. Let stand in a warm place until doubled in volume.

Combine the butter, egg yolks and 10 dag sugar in a mixer bowl. Beat until light and fluffy, scraping the bowl occasionally. Combine the heated milk, rum, lemon peel and salt in a bowl and mix well. Add 3/4 of the milk mixture to the butter mixture and mix well. Stir in the flour and yeast mixture. Add the remaining milk mixture gradually and mix well. (The quantity of milk used varies according to the quality of the flour. Use all the milk with very fine-grain flour; use less with inferior-quality flour.) Beat vigorously with a wooden spoon until the dough is smooth and separates easily from the spoon and bowl. Let stand, covered, in a warm place until doubled in bulk.

Roll to the thickness of your little finger on a lightly floured surface. Spread with the Walnut Filling to within 5 centimeters (1.96 inches) of the edge. Roll gently, but make sure there are no air pockets left in the roll. For easy handling, roll the dough on a dry linen cloth lightly dusted with flour. Grease the baking dish; sprinkle with bread crumbs. Arrange the potica seam side down in the prepared dish. Let stand, covered with a linen cloth, in a warm place until doubled in bulk.

Bake at 200 degrees Celsius (392 degrees Fahrenheit) for 1 hour; tent with foil if needed to prevent overbrowning. Remove to a serving platter immediately. Sprinkle with superfine sugar. Let stand, lightly covered with a cloth, until cool. Traditionally potica is baked one day in advance of serving.

WALNUT FILLING

.125 (.52 cup) liter milk

30 dag (10.58 ounces) ground walnuts

15 dag (5.29 ounces) sugar

2 tablespoons dry bread crumbs

3 dag (1.05 ounces) butter, softened

3 tablespoons whipping cream

2 egg yolks, lightly beaten

$1/2$ teaspoon cinnamon

$1/2$ teaspoon ground cloves

2 eggs whites

Scald the milk in a saucepan. Stir in the walnuts. Stir in the sugar, bread crumbs, butter, whipping cream, egg yolks, cinnamon and cloves. Beat the egg whites in a mixer bowl until stiff. Fold into the milk mixture. Substitute ground hazelnuts for the walnuts for Hazelnut Filling.

TARRAGON FILLING

10 dag (3.5 ounces) butter, softened

10 dag (3.5 ounces) sugar

3 egg yolks

$1/2$ cup chopped fresh tarragon

Beat the butter, sugar and egg yolks in a mixer bowl until light and fluffy. Stir in the tarragon.

Walnut Filling, Tarragon Filling or Chocolate Filling

Bread crumbs

Vanilla-flavor superfine sugar

Continued on page 166

CHOCOLATE FILLING

20 dag (7.05 ounces) butter, softened

20 dag (7.05 ounces) sugar

4 eggs

25 dag (8.81 ounces) chocolate, melted, or baking cocoa

25 dag (8.81 ounces) chopped almonds

Beat the butter, sugar and eggs in a mixer bowl until light and fluffy. Add the chocolate, beating until blended. Stir in the almonds.

DR. EVA BAHOVEC   LJUBJANA, SLOVENIJA

FOOD FOR THOUGHT

The secret of a good potica is in the appropriate dough, and the secret of the dough is in the flour. Use only high-quality, very dry fine grain wheat flour. Make sure that the flour is heated. Making good potica requires a bit of suffering. You should prepare it in a very hot kitchen, otherwise the yeast or the dough may "catch cold" and the potica won't rise properly. Potica is traditionally baked in a round toroidal ceramic mold. But whatever you use, make sure the mold is a high one—potica is supposed to rise a lot. For good potica, the proportions of the height of the mold versus its width should be at least two to one.

CHILDREN IN THE KITCHEN

*High/Scope disseminates research findings and services through
training programs, conferences, and publications.*

YIELD: 1 SERVING

BLENDER APPLESAUCE

This recipe is a good alternative to the stove-top method.

1 Granny Smith apple
Cinnamon-sugar to taste
1 to 3 tablespoons water

Core the apple. Cut the apple into pieces and place in a blender container. Add the cinnamon-sugar.

Process until blended. Add enough of the water to make of the desired consistency, processing constantly. Spoon into a serving bowl.

KELLY HAMILTON   PITTSBURGH, PENNSYLVANIA

FOOD FOR THOUGHT

May use your favorite kind of apple for this recipe and may peel the apple if desired.

NO-LID POPCORN

YIELD: VARIABLE

My students love this snack. It is fun to make and eat.

Let the children sit on the floor on the edge of a large sheet. Place the popcorn popper in the center of the sheet. Add the oil and popcorn kernels to the popcorn popper.

Wait and listen for the popcorn to pop, keeping children away from the hot popper. Measure and compare how high the popcorn pops. Eat the popcorn after it has finished popping.

BECKY CARSWELL   WOODBRIDGE, VIRGINIA

Vegetable oil
Popcorn kernels

169

YIELD: 12 SERVINGS

3/4 cup apple juice

1 (3-ounce) package
flavored gelatin

1 envelope unflavored
gelatin

3/4 cup apple juice, chilled

5 ice cubes

SLIPPERY SNAKES

Bring 3/4 cup apple juice to a boil in a saucepan and remove from heat. Add the flavored gelatin. Stir until the gelatin is dissolved. Soften the unflavored gelatin in 3/4 cup cold apple juice in a bowl. Add to the hot gelatin mixture, stirring constantly until the gelatin is dissolved. Add the ice cubes and stir until melted. Chill for 15 minutes or until partially set.

Divide the gelatin into 2 equal portions. Place each portion in a sealable food storage bag and seal. Cut 1/4 inch off the corner of each storage bag. Pipe the gelatin onto a foil-lined baking sheet, forming "snakes." Chill for 2 hours or until set.

BECKY CARSWELL   WOODBRIDGE, VIRGINIA

TRAIL MIX

YIELD: VARIABLE

A good way to use leftover snacks and also a good way to have each child share a favorite snack.

Place each ingredient in a large serving bowl and provide a spoon with each one for dipping. Give each child a clean yogurt cup with a lid.

Let the children spoon some of their favorite snacks into their cups. Cover with the lids and shake well to mix.

KELLY HAMILTON   PITTSBURGH, PENNSYLVANIA

Goldfish crackers
Bite-size pretzels
Cereal
Peanuts
Gummy bears
Raisins

YIELD: 30 SERVINGS

5 *pounds pasta, cooked, drained*

3 *pounds smoked turkey, chopped*

3 *pounds sour cream*

3 *pounds shredded Cheddar cheese*

4 *pounds cucumbers, chopped*

2 *quarts salsa*

PASTA BY DESIGN

Divide the pasta into 4 portions and place each portion in a 2-quart serving bowl. Divide the smoked turkey into 4 portions and place each portion in a 1-cup serving bowl. Repeat the process with the sour cream, Cheddar cheese, cucumbers and salsa.

Set up 4 separate food lines containing the 6 food choices. Let the children go through the lines creating their own pasta lunch. Encourage them to try all the foods by talking to them about each food as they are preparing their plates.

KASENA DAILEY   BEAVERTON, OREGON

CHICKEN NOODLE SOUP

YIELD: VARIABLE

A good way for children to help make soup without using a stove.

Let the children pour enough water into a slow cooker to fill 3/4 full. Let the children unwrap the bouillon cubes and add to the water. Let them chop the chicken and add the chicken and pasta to the slow cooker.

Cook, covered, on High for 1 hour or until heated through, stirring every 15 minutes. Ladle into individual serving bowls.

KELLY HAMILTON   PITTSBURGH, PENNSYLVANIA

Bouillon cubes to taste
Cooked chicken or turkey
Alphabet noodles or any favorite pasta

YIELD: 20 SERVINGS

DINOSAUR SOUP

1 large meaty beef knuckle
  or leg bone

8 carrots

1/2 stalk celery with leaves

3 to 4 potatoes

1/4 to 1/2 head cabbage, cut
  into thin slices

2 onions, coarsely chopped

1 large can tomatoes

1 small can tomato paste

  Salt and pepper to taste

1/2 cup alphabet noodles
  (optional)

Children love dinosaurs. Making Dinosaur Soup was one of their favorite projects when we were studying dinosaurs. The children learned about the vegetables that went into the soup and we discussed that some of the vegetables were roots. We also discussed that dinosaurs probably ate roots, flowers, stalks, leaves, etc. Adding the alphabet noodles really helped encourage them to eat every drop of the soup.

Rinse and dry the bone. Cut any meat from the bone and crack the bone if possible. Brown the bone in a small amount of vegetable oil in a stockpot.

Divide the children into groups. Let one group of children scrape the carrots. Let another group cut the carrots into slices using a butter knife. Let one group of children rinse the celery and cut into bite-size pieces using a butter knife. Let one group of children scrub and peel the potatoes using a butter knife. An adult can cut the potatoes into strips and then the children can cut the potato strips into bite-size pieces using a butter knife.

Let each group add their vegetables to the stockpot. Add the cabbage and onions. Let the children help open the cans of tomatoes and tomato paste. Let the children chop the tomatoes with a butter knife. Add the chopped tomatoes and tomato paste to the stockpot. Sprinkle with salt and pepper. Add enough water to cover all the ingredients. Bring to a boil and reduce heat. Simmer for 1 hour and 50 minutes. Add the alphabet noodles. Cook for 10 minutes longer.

CAROL SUE RAITT   FRANKLIN SPRINGS, NEW YORK

Indian Fry Bread

Yield: 12 large

or

20 small servings

It's a little messy, but fun to eat.

Mix the flour, baking powder and salt in a bowl. Cut in the shortening until the mixture resembles coarse crumbs. Stir in the warm water, forming a soft dough. Knead the dough on a lightly floured surface a few times. Shape into a ball and cover with plastic wrap. Let the dough rest for 20 minutes.

Shape the dough into 1-inch balls. Pat into 6-inch circles. Punch a hole through the center of each circle using your finger.

Pour the vegetable oil to a depth of 2 inches in a large skillet. Heat the vegetable oil to 375 degrees. Add the circles to the hot vegetable oil. Fry for 1 minute or until golden and crisp. Turn the circles over to the other side. Fry for 30 seconds. Drain the bread on paper towels. Sift the confectioners' sugar over the bread or drizzle with the honey.

Marilyn Alarcon   Pioneer, California

- 2 cups flour
- 2 tablespoons baking powder
- 1 teaspoon salt
- 2 tablespoons shortening
- 2/3 cup warm water
  Vegetable oil for frying
  Sifted confectioners' sugar or honey (optional)

Food for Thought

This can be made into an Indian Taco by layering cooked meat, grated cheese, chopped tomatoes and sliced lettuce on top of the bread. My students enjoy making this for their Thanksgiving feast, when "traveling the Oregon Trail," or during their "49er migration to California," or before "Pow Wow."

YIELD: 12 TO 15 SERVINGS

3 (10-count) cans butter
   biscuits
1 cup sugar
3 tablespoons cinnamon
1/2 cup margarine
3/4 cup packed brown sugar

GREAT-GRANDFATHER'S MONKEY BREAD

In memory of Great-Grandfather Wayne Hertz. He used to dunk these in his coffee.

Cut each biscuit dough round into quarters. Add to a mixture of the sugar and cinnamon in a bowl and coat well. Drop into a bundt pan. Melt the margarine in a saucepan. Add the brown sugar. Heat until the brown sugar dissolves, stirring constantly. Pour over the dough in the prepared pan.

Bake at 350 degrees for 30 to 40 minutes or until the bread tests done. Invert immediately onto a serving plate.

BETSY AND CALLIE COLE   MONROE, MICHIGAN

NUTTY MONKEY BREAD

YIELD: 15 SERVINGS

We make this recipe during "animal" month. Everyone loves it.

Combine the margarine and brown sugar in a large microwave-safe bowl. Microwave on High until the margarine is melted. Stir in the nuts.

Cut the biscuit dough rounds into quarters using kitchen scissors. Add to the brown sugar mixture and stir well to coat. Pour into an 8x8-inch baking pan sprayed with nonstick cooking spray. Bake at 350 degrees for 20 minutes.

SUZANNE F. CAMPESE   PEMBROKE PINES, FLORIDA

1/2 cup margarine
1 cup packed brown sugar
1 cup chopped nuts
2 (10-count) cans biscuits

YIELD: 12 SERVINGS

1¹/₂ *cups unsweetened berries*

2 *bananas*

1 *cup juice-pack crushed pineapple*

1 *(6-ounce) can frozen orange juice concentrate*

2¹/₂ *cups plain low-fat yogurt*

¹/₄ *cup honey*

1¹/₂ *cups crushed ice*

F R U I T   S H E R B E T

Combine the berries, bananas, pineapple, orange juice concentrate, yogurt, honey and ice in a blender container. Process until well blended.

Pour into twelve 5-ounce paper cups. Freeze until firm. Remove from the freezer and let soften before serving.

KASENA DAILEY   BEAVERTON, OREGON

RAINBOW PUDDING

Children love this dessert.

Combine the pudding mix and milk in a bowl and mix well. Let stand for a few minutes until thick.

Divide the pudding into 4 bowls. Add a drop of red, blue and yellow food coloring to each bowl. Stir and watch the magic.

BECKY CARSWELL   WOODBRIDGE, VIRGINIA

YIELD: 4 SERVINGS

1 (4-ounce) package vanilla instant pudding mix
2 cups cold milk
Red, blue and yellow food coloring

181

YIELD: 15 SERVINGS

1 (2-layer) package yellow
  cake mix
1 (4-ounce) package
  chocolate instant pudding
  mix
1/2 cup vegetable oil
1 cup sour cream
4 eggs
1 tablespoon vanilla extract
2 cups chocolate chips
1 cup chopped nuts

CHOCOLATE CHIP BUNDT CAKE

*As a third-grader, my daughter, Elizabeth, won second prize at the
library bake-off with this recipe.*

Combine the cake mix, pudding mix, vegetable oil, sour cream, eggs and vanilla in a large mixer bowl. Beat for 5 minutes or until the batter is thick. Stir in the chocolate chips and nuts. Spoon into a greased and floured bundt pan.

Bake at 350 degrees for 55 to 60 minutes or until the cake tests done. Cool in the pan for 30 minutes. Invert onto a wire rack to cool completely.

MARLENE BARR   YPSILANTI, MICHIGAN

CREAM CHEESE MINTS

YIELD: 1/2 TO 3/4 POUND

Beat the cream cheese and confectioners' sugar in a bowl until smooth. Add the flavoring and mix well. Tint with food coloring. Knead on a surface coated with confectioners' sugar, adding additional confectioners' sugar if needed.

Shape into balls and roll in the sugar. Press into candy molds or crisscross with the tines of a fork.

KELLY HAMILTON   PITTSBURGH, PENNSYLVANIA

FOOD FOR THOUGHT

I use Lorain oils for the flavoring in this recipe. You may omit the cream cheese and use 1/2 cup melted butter and increase the confectioners' sugar to 4 cups. Add a small amount of milk if needed for the desired consistency and continue as above.

3 ounces cream cheese, softened
2 1/2 cups confectioners' sugar
4 drops of favorite mint flavoring
Food coloring
Sugar

YIELD: 36 SERVINGS

16 ounces miniature
    semisweet chocolate chips
1 (14-ounce) can sweetened
    condensed milk
2 teaspoons vanilla extract

EASY FUDGE

*One Thanksgiving my daughter made a turkey-shaped centerpiece out of batches
of white and dark chocolate fudge. Ever since, she has considered this fudge to be
an essential part of all special occasions.*

Combine the miniature chocolate chips and condensed milk in a microwave-safe bowl.
Microwave on High for 1 minute and stir. Microwave for 2 minutes longer or until the
miniature chocolate chips are melted, stirring every 30 seconds to make sure the
chocolate is melting evenly. Add the vanilla.

Beat until the chocolate is thoroughly combined and the mixture is smooth. Pour
immediately into a buttered 9x9-inch pan. Chill for several hours or until firm. Cut
into squares.

NANCY BRICKMAN–HIGH/SCOPE EDITOR   YPSILANTI, MICHIGAN

FOOD FOR THOUGHT

*Any form of sweet chocolate (such as milk or white chocolate) will work, but the
miniature chocolate chips are the easiest to work with because they melt most evenly.*

AGGRESSION COOKIES

YIELD: 1 1/2 DOZEN

A great cookie to make with children when they are learning about emotions.

Combine the oats, brown sugar, flour, butter, baking powder, cinnamon and nutmeg in a large bowl. Use your hands to twist, fold, squeeze and beat. The more mixing the better.

Shape the dough into balls. Place 2 inches apart on a greased cookie sheet. Bake at 350 degrees for 10 to 12 minutes or until golden brown. Cool on a wire rack.

BECKY CARSWELL   WOODBRIDGE, VIRGINIA

3 cups rolled oats
1 1/2 cups packed brown sugar
1 1/2 cups flour
1 1/2 cups butter, softened
1 1/2 teaspoons baking powder
1/2 teaspoon cinnamon
1/2 teaspoon nutmeg

YIELD: 4 SERVINGS

ELEPHANT EARS

1 *stick pie crust mix*
3 *tablespoons hot water*
2 *tablespoons sugar*
2 *teaspoons cinnamon*

Break the pie crust stick into little pieces in a bowl. Add the hot water. Mix with a fork until a soft dough forms. Shape with lightly floured hands into a big ball on a lightly floured surface.

Divide the ball into 4 portions. Shape each portion into a ball. Press each to flatten 1/4 inch thick. Place on an ungreased cookie sheet. Sprinkle with a mixture of the sugar and cinnamon. Bake at 350 degrees for 20 minutes or until brown. Cool on a wire rack.

BECKY CARSWELL   WOODBRIDGE, VIRGINIA

LAYERED COOKIE BARS

My students enjoy making this recipe so much that they experiment with other toppings also. They've tried everything from M & M's Chocolate Candies to cake decorations and jelly beans.

Pat the cookie dough into a 9x13-inch baking pan sprayed with nonstick cooking spray. Bake at 350 degrees for 10 minutes.

Pour the condensed milk over the hot partially baked layer. Sprinkle with the chocolate chips, coconut and nuts. Press the toppings lightly into the condensed milk. Bake for 15 minutes or until the edges are light brown. Let stand until completely cooled. Cut into bars.

MARILYN ALARCON   PIONEER, CALIFORNIA

FOOD FOR THOUGHT

May add 1 cup butterscotch chips or peanut butter chips with the chocolate chips and use peanut butter cookie dough instead of sugar cookie dough.

1 (20-ounce) package refrigerated sugar cookie dough

1 (14-ounce) can sweetened condensed milk

1 cup chocolate chips

1 cup flaked coconut

1 cup chopped nuts

Fudge Oatmeal Cookies

2 cups sugar

1/2 cup baking cocoa

1/2 cup margarine

1/2 cup milk

1/2 cup smooth or crunchy
   peanut butter

1 teaspoon vanilla extract

3 cups rolled oats

A family favorite.

Bring the sugar, baking cocoa, margarine and milk to a boil in a large saucepan. Boil for 2 minutes, stirring constantly. Remove from heat. Add the peanut butter and vanilla and mix well. Stir in the oats.

Drop by teaspoonfuls onto waxed paper. Let stand until cool.

Jan Gifford—High/Scope Elementary Division Secretary
Ypsilanti, Michigan

INDIVIDUAL RICE KRISPIES TREATS

YIELD: VARIABLE

1/2 cup butter
1 (10-ounce) package
   miniature marshmallows
Rice Krispies

*I adapted the traditional recipe to include all children and to make it a
more hands-on approach for the children to make their own individual portions.*

Combine the butter and marshmallows in a microwave-safe bowl. Microwave on High
until melted. Spoon several tablespoonfuls of the mixture into small individual bowls.
Add enough of the cereal gradually to each bowl to form a mixture that is very stiff but
not dry, stirring constantly.

Shape each portion into a ball and flatten slightly. Cut into desired shapes using
cookie cutters. Let stand until firm. Store individually wrapped in plastic wrap.

KELLY HAMILTON   PITTSBURGH, PENNSYLVANIA

NONEDIBLE PLAY DOUGH

4 cups flour
1 cup salt
1/2 cup cream of tartar
4 cups water
1/4 cup vegetable oil
Food coloring

Mix the flour, salt and cream of tartar in a medium saucepan. Add a mixture of the water, vegetable oil and food coloring.

Cook over medium heat for 3 to 5 minutes or until it forms a ball, stirring constantly. Knead on a lightly floured surface until smooth. Store in an airtight container or sealable plastic bag.

CAROL MARKLEY—HIGH/SCOPE DEMONSTRATION PRESCHOOL TEACHER
YPSILANTI, MICHIGAN

FOOD FOR THOUGHT

The mixture will look like a big "globby" mess while cooking, but continue stirring until it forms a ball. You may omit the cream of tartar and use an additional 1/4 cup flour and 1/4 cup salt.

N O N E D I B L E   P U F F Y   P A I N T

*This is great for vision-impaired children because once the
paint dries, they can feel their designs.*

Combine the flour, salt and water in a bowl and mix well. Add the tempera paint and
mix well. Pour into clean empty glue bottles.

Let the children make their designs on paper using the puffy paint and let dry.

MONA TIMMONS   FALLON, NEVADA

1 *cup flour*

1 *cup salt*

1 *cup water*

*Few drops of tempera
paint*

191

N O N E D I B L E   F L U B B E R   S L I M E

Warm water

Glue

1/4 to 1/2 teaspoon borax

1/4 cup warm water

This recipe was presented at a High/Scope International Registry Conference session entitled "Play and Be Playful: Remembering Our Own Child."

Mix equal parts warm water and glue in a large bowl. Give each child a small bowl. Have each child measure and add 1/4 to 1/2 teaspoon borax and 1/4 cup warm water to the small bowl and mix well.

The contents of the small bowl are then dumped by each child into the large bowl and each child mixes well. The more borax added the stiffer it gets.

MONA TIMMONS   FALLON, NEVADA

OUTDOOR COOKING METHODS

*High/Scope's Institute for IDEAS boosts the achievement
and career aspirations of disadvantaged teens.*

At High/Scope's Institute for IDEAS, a summer program for adolescents, outdoor cooking is a time-honored tradition. We hope that you will enjoy the following instructions for foil cooking and reflector oven baking.

F O I L   C O O K I N G

Since the first cook used fire, we have been cooking on coals. First, we slapped the food on the burning embers to enhance the natural flavors. Later, it was discovered that by wrapping the food in leaves to seal it, palatability of whatever was being cooked was increased by using steam to soften the tough fibers and retain the natural juices. This method also enabled us to add herbs and other ingredients to further enhance the taste. In foil cooking, the aluminum foil serves the same purpose as the leaves did originally.

First, place whatever you want to cook on the shiny side of a 14-inch piece of aluminum foil. Fold it into a well-sealed package by overlapping to lock the seams and make it steam-tight. Don't put more than two servings in a packet, because it may separate at the seams and tear if too full.

Second, prepare the fire so the cooking temperature will be around 375 degrees. Test this by placing the back of your hand near the intended cooking site and counting to four. If you can count higher, move more coals to the area to increase the heat. If you have to move your hand away earlier, spread the coals to reduce the heat.

How do you tell when your food is done? Stick a fork or knife into the packet and judge if there is resistance, or carefully open the foil and taste a piece. Most of the time your foil dinner will be done to perfection in about 15 minutes. If need be, cooking can be hastened by increasing the heat and every 5 minutes moving the packet end over end and upside down.

What should you put in your packet? Following are some suggestions that you might like to try, but your imagination and the size of the item should be the only limitations on what to cook.

FOIL-COOKING COMBINATIONS

CURRIED CARROTS

Cut 3 carrots into bite-size pieces. Combine the carrots, 2 teaspoons curry powder, garlic salt to taste, 2 tablespoons margarine, and salt and pepper to taste in a foil-packet. Cook until the carrots are tender-crisp.

BAKED POTATOES

Scrub and rinse 1 medium potato. Wrap in foil. Cook for 40 to 60 minutes or until the potato tests done. Test for doneness by squeezing the potato. If soft, remove from heat. Potatoes cook at varying rates.

GROUND BEEF STEW

Combine 4 ounces ground beef, mixed vegetables to taste, Worcestershire sauce to taste, minced garlic to taste, and salt and pepper to taste in a foil-packet. Cook until the ground beef is cooked through.

CARRICK LEGRISMITH-HIGH/SCOPE CAMP AND CONFERENCE CENTER
CLINTON, MICHIGAN

REFLECTOR OVEN

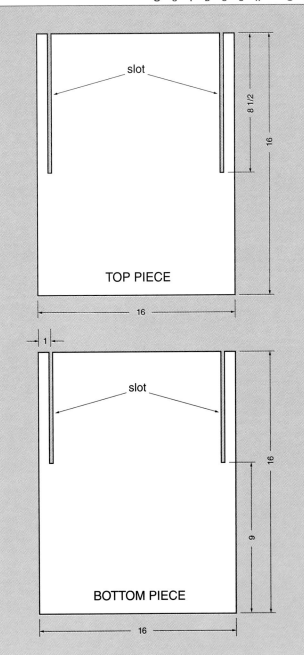

TOP PIECE

8 1/2

16

16

slot

BOTTOM PIECE

1

16

9

16

slot

NOTES:

Use 12 gauge aluminum
Slots: cut width of metal + 1/16"
Cut 4 metal bars 18" long
Holes cut to fit the diameter of the metal bars
Cooking pan = 9" x 12" x 2"

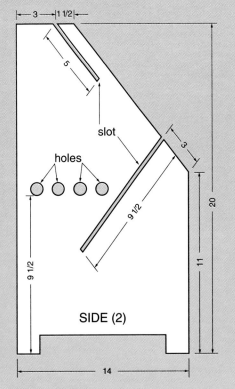

SIDE (2)

3 · 1 1/2

5

slot

holes

3

9 1/2

20

11

9 1/2

14

R E F L E C T O R   O V E N   B A K I N G

THE OVEN

A good reflector oven has proper supports for the cooking pan, space for limited air circulation behind the pan while in the oven, and proper reflecting angles. Pictured on page 199 is a solid aluminum portable oven. The drawing, at left, gives the dimensions, gauge, and length of support poles. It can be easily made with a standard electric saw and a file to round the edges. The steel poles happen to be stainless steel, but any steel bar will work as well.

A low-rimmed rectangular pan is also necessary. While almost any pan that will fit in the oven is adequate, a 9x13-inch baking pan is typical. A heavy-gauge aluminum pan with a nonstick surface is best.

THE FIRE

In a conventional oven, the air is heated and the hot air then cooks the food. In contrast, reflector oven baking uses radiant heat. The heat waves from the fire hit the shiny surface of the metal oven and reflect onto the food. In order for this to be successful, the fire must be almost as high as the oven so that heat is radiated against both the top and the bottom aluminum reflecting surfaces. It should also be as wide as the oven so that the cooking will be even. Fire stakes can be pushed into the ground in order to hold the pile of burning wood vertically and ensure that the flame is as hot at the top as at the bottom. A good reflector oven fire is slow burning and should be made from hardwood, such as birch, maple, oak, ash, or beech. Softwoods, such as pines and other trees with needles, burn too quickly to provide the slow, even heat necessary for baking. The oven should be placed 6 to 8 inches from the fire.

THE TEMPERATURE

To determine the oven temperature, begin by holding the back of your hand beside the forward legs of the oven at the height of the pan. If you can hold your hand there for 3 to 4 seconds, the temperature estimate is 400 degrees. If you have to move your hand away earlier, the fire is too hot and the oven should be moved back. If you can hold your hand beside the legs for a count of 5 to 6, it is approximately 250 degrees. In this case, you either need a hotter fire or the oven should be moved closer. As your item is baking, you must watch to see that the temperature is maintained by tending the fire or moving the oven. As with standard baking, a toothpick or twig can be used to determine whether the item has cooked sufficiently.

THE RECIPES

Any standard indoor cooking recipes that call for baking can be done in the reflector oven. Because building and tending the fire require a great deal of time and effort, many people prefer to use store-bought mixes in order to minimize preparation time. Brownies, corn bread, biscuits, cakes, and pies are all easily prepared with mixes. Several of these require an egg or two and all require a slightly greased pan. Bought at the last minute, a carefully wrapped and insulated carton of eggs will last for several days if the weather is not too warm.

Other things can be baked as well. Canned meats are already cooked and so only need to be reheated with some liquid added. Biscuit dough can be baked on top of the meat to prepare like a shepherd's pie.

Reflector oven baking is mostly art with a few rules. Each time you do it is an adventure requiring skill and timing. But with a level pan, a high vertical fire, careful mixing of the ingredients, proper temperature, and a healthy appetite, you are in for a satisfying experience.

DAVID WEIKART—HIGH/SCOPE PRESIDENT   YPSILANTI, MICHIGAN

CONTRIBUTOR INDEX

INDEX

ORDER INFORMATION

HIGH/SCOPE
600 North River Street
Ypsilanti, Michigan 48198-2898

Phone/Fax
800-40-PRESS
800-442-4FAX

	Qty.	Total
Stone Soup (cat. # D1000)—$18.95 each		
Michigan residents add 6% sales tax—$1.14 each		
Postage and Handling—$4.95 each		
Total		

Ship to:

Name

Street Address

City   State   Zip

Daytime Phone (   )   Nighttime Phone (   )

Method of Payment: ☐ VISA   ☐ MasterCard   ☐ AMEX

Card Number   Expiration Date

Signature

Please make checks payable to High/Scope.